D1551430

BOB FITRAKIS

The Fitrakis Files: Free Byrd & Other Cries For Justice

EDITED BY BRIAN LINDAMOOD

A COLUMBUS INSTITUTE FOR CONTEMPORARY JOURNALISM BOOK

PUBLISHED BY COLUMBUS ALIVE PUBLISHING

*This book is dedicated to the memory
of John William Byrd Jr.,
the Byrd family,
and to my mentor, Marty Yant*

Acknowledgements

This second collection of writings in the "Fitrakis Files" series reflects a decade of death penalty investigative reporting and other inquiries into Ohio's prison-industrial complex. I am indebted to many people for the information contained in this volume.

First and foremost, I am indebted to the late John William Byrd Jr., who corresponded with me for seven years from his Death Row cell he called "the cage," and who spoke to me thoughtfully and, I believe, honestly, by phone during the last months of his life. In the seven years of communication Johnny never contradicted himself and steadfastly maintained his innocence regarding the night of the tragic murder of Monte Tewksbury. While I wholeheartedly agree that the memory of Mr. Tewksbury must be honored, I fail to see how executing the wrong man honored Tewksbury's memory in any way.

The first time I spoke with Johnny, he told me of his ambition to be a writer. Having read numerous letters from Johnny over the years, I can attest that he was a fine writer. The readers of this volume may judge for themselves, since we have included a piece by Johnny, titled "The Last Mile," about his brush with execution in 1994 (see page 233). He was also a gifted poet and artist, an aficionado of

vii

Shakespeare and fluent in various languages that he had taught himself on Death Row.

In my last conversation with Johnny just prior to his execution, he was quite calm and composed and mostly concerned that I might become depressed after he was killed. "Look, they're going to kill me, brother. You've got to stay strong and tell the story. Don't worry about me, I'll be fine. I don't want to spend the rest of my life in this cage," he told me.

I never got to meet Byrd face to face, although a request was put in by the Ohio Public Defender's Office. Ohio prison officials claimed I would pose a security threat on Death Row. Johnny agreed, saying, "You are a threat to them, brother. You tell the truth."

The closest I came to seeing Johnny Byrd was a last-minute attempt with Columbus attorney Cliff Arnebeck and the Reverend Gary Witte the night before Johnny was to be transferred to the Lucasville death chamber. We raced to the Mansfield prison to serve subpoenas on the warden in hopes of taking Johnny's deposition for a possible wrongful death lawsuit against the state of Ohio. A phalanx of prison guards and the captain of the guards stared down an assertive Arnebeck, who demanded that Johnny be allowed to talk to the Reverend. I served as Arnebeck's law clerk and researcher. I like to think that the guards told Johnny that those who believed in his innocence were staying strong and fighting to the last for justice in Ohio.

I'm deeply indebted to Mary Ray, John Byrd's mother, who is fond of calling me "honey" and mistakenly insisting that I'm handsome. Johnny was always worried about his mother who, until that fateful day, February 19, 2002, believed "my baby's coming home." Both Mary and Johnny's sister, Kim Hamer, graciously allowed me access to boxes of documents on Johnny's case as well as correspondence and other material he had written throughout his life. Both consented to numerous interviews, in Mary's case in between hospital stays. I hope this collection meets with their approval.

Dick Vickers and the Ohio Public Defender's Office, unlike the Prosecutor's Office, opened up their public records on the Byrd case for countless hours of perusal. Vickers patiently endured the questions of a reporter trying to digest volumes of information on a short deadline. I am grateful to him for his courtesy, and his courage, which was revealed in the files.

My mentor, Marty Yant, the author of *Presumed Guilty*, co-wrote several articles in this collection, all concerning the Byrd case. He generously allowed these to be re-printed in this volume. In the last desperate days of the Byrd case, Yant worked tirelessly as an investigator, uncovering shocking evidence long concealed by the Hamilton County Prosecutor's Office. In 2002, Yant and I, along with Jamie Pietras, won the first-place award for Best Criminal Justice Reporting from the Ohio Society of Professional Journalists for our investigation into the John Byrd death penalty case. That collective reporting is encapsulated in this volume. I only regret Johnny is not here to share in the honor.

I owe a debt to Jamie Pietras as well, a brilliant reporter now finishing his master's degree at the Columbia School of Journalism. Pietras' great skill was getting people to talk who I couldn't even get to answer my phone calls. Pietras constantly turned the Byrd case over in his mind and came up with the original "fourth man" theory even before we were aware of the existence of Bobby Pottinger, an early suspect in the murder.

Ida Strong and Dan Cahill of the Prisoner Advocacy Network were more than mere advocates for Johnny Byrd. Both provided key information on not only the Byrd case, but several other stories in this collection. Ida also assisted by typing parts of this manuscript and acting as the head nudge in pushing the volume's completion.

Other Death Row inmates and prisoners were helpful in the preparation of this volume, particularly John Spirko, George Skatzes and John Perotti.

On the general topic of the death penalty, I would like to thank Howard Tolley, an extraordinary human rights scholar and activist; Professor John Quigley, whom I had the privilege of studying human rights with at the Ohio State University College of Law and who was a resource for some of these stories; Dr. Jonathon Groner, who provided essential information on lethal injection that proved invaluable; and Michael Manley of Central Ohioans Against Executions.

I would also like to acknowledge the family of Michael Hiles, Michael Dray, the late Little Rock Reed and the Native American Indian Center of Central Ohio, which helped arrange calls from Reed during the time he was somewhere in the Southwest while the Ohio Attorney General sought his extradition.

I would like to thank Percy Squire, owner of the radio station WSMZ FM, who allowed me to accept collect calls from Ohio inmates while live on the air before the state of Ohio claimed the calls to my talk show posed a threat to prison security.

David Schalliol assembled computer documents of the *Columbus Alive* writings used in this book, and for that I am thankful. Reg Dyck proofread key portions of this manuscript on short notice just prior to deadline. I am indebted to him for his last-minute heroics.

I want to express my gratitude to Holly Vaske for not only her cover design of this second volume, but her stunning work on the first volume, *The Fitrakis Files: Spooks, Nukes & Nazis*. Most importantly, I thank *Alive*'s dutiful and long-suffering editor, Brian Lindamood, who worked tediously to compile this collection. Without Lindamood's efforts, these writings on Ohio's Death Row and the prison-industrial complex would have never been put into book form.

Finally, I would like to thank my wife, Suzanne Patzer, who edited, proofread and endured this project, not only because of her love for me, but equally because of her strong commitment to social justice.

Contents

POST SCRIPT

Introduction

BY BRIAN LINDAMOOD

Rich people do not receive the death penalty in Ohio. This state only executes its poorest citizens. One hundred percent of the inmates on Death Row are indigent, unable to afford their own attorneys.

African-Americans are overwhelmingly sentenced to death by the state of Ohio. About 50 percent of the 200-plus inmates on Death Row are black, even though only 12 percent of Ohio residents are black.

Ohio kills the mentally ill, as it did when Wilford Berry was put to death in 1999, and until very recently the U.S. was one of only a handful of countries in the world to execute the mentally retarded. The United States is also in good company when it comes to executing children. The only other countries that put to death their juvenile delinquents are Congo, Iran and Pakistan.

Crime and punishment is never pretty. But what's most upsetting about the death penalty, the ultimate irrevocable punishment, is that it's applied so unequally.

For proof of that, take a drive outside of Columbus, just a few miles in any direction. Once you cross the county line, your chances of receiving the death penalty are greatly diminished. That's because capital punishment is rarely used outside of Ohio's major metropolitan areas. Forty-six of Ohio's 88 counties have not used the death penalty since it was reinstated in 1981.

Even when society must be harsh—and it should be harsh when it deals with criminals—it should always be fair. That's what justice is. Blind. Equal. Fair.

The problem with the death penalty in Ohio is that it's just not fair. We kill the poor, never the rich. We kill blacks far more than whites. We kill the mentally ill and children, the weakest members of society who may not be cognizant of their crimes or, at very least, most deserve a chance at rehabilitation.

Far from fair, the death penalty is cruel and capricious. But it is still supported by a majority of Ohio residents.

Why? It's not cost. The death penalty is far more expensive to implement—twice as expensive, in the case of Wilford Berry—than is life in prison.

Security? Life in prison without the possibility of parole would seem just as effective a way to keep a killer off the streets.

Deterring crime? Hardly. The death penalty is applied so unevenly that criminals might as well take their chances with the Death Row lottery. A rich white woman is never going to receive the death penalty in Ohio—so don't let it deter you from committing capital murder. If you commit a capital crime in rural Ohio, chances are you won't end up on Death Row either. The "deterrence" would only apply to poor black men in Cleveland, Columbus and Cincinnati.

Retribution? Since inmates sit on Ohio's Death Row for decades, their eventual execution would seem to be little solace for the grieving families of victims. Even Ohio Supreme Court Justice Paul Pfeifer told *Columbus Alive* that the extraordinary lag time between inmates' sentencing and execution undermines the primary justification for the death penalty.

The death penalty doesn't seem justifiable under any of the usual standards of the criminal justice system. But there is a simple reason why most Ohioans still support execution: Vengeance.

The death penalty satisfies our societal bloodlust. We feel better about ourselves when we can kill our most dangerous outcasts. Locking them up for life—and making society just as safe—isn't good enough. We want to see the bad guys fry.

And so what if a few good guys get in the way.

This, though, is really the problem, isn't it? What if a good guy did get in the way?

Innocent men trapped on Death Row hasn't become the issue in Ohio it has in other states. Illinois freed 13 people from Death Row after DNA tests proved their innocence. Score one for modern technology, but this begs the question: What if this had happened 10 or even five years ago? Thirteen innocent men would have been executed. For all we know, innocent men were executed five or 10 years ago in states across the country.

And an innocent man may have been executed in Ohio last year, when John Byrd was put to death even though no physical evidence tied him to the crime he supposedly committed.

Bob Fitrakis closely followed Byrd's case for nearly a decade, reporting on the seemingly endless series of judicial travesties in the *Columbus Free Press* and *Columbus Alive.* Those reports are reprinted in this volume, along with other probes into the criminal-justice system, and with the

invaluable contributions of reporters Martin Yant and Jamie
Pietras. We've tried to make a difference—exposing injustice where we've seen it—but, unfortunately, this book
doesn't have a happy ending. Not yet, anyway.

The justice system is a human system, always based on
the passion of human prosecutors, the consideration of
human judges and the best judgment of 12 ordinary citizens. It is not a perfect system. The calculated accuracy of
DNA testing notwithstanding, men are still sent to Death
Row in Ohio based solely on circumstantial evidence.
Mistakes have been and will be made.

But wrongful imprisonment can be corrected, the jailhouse doors opened with society's apologies. Wrongful
execution cannot be corrected. The death of an innocent
man isn't punishment, it's state-sanctioned murder.

In an enlightened, intelligent society, we simply cannot
take that chance. The risk is too great—the implications of
a mistake too horrible to consider. Can you imagine the terror of being strapped to a gurney and lethally injected for
a crime you did not commit? But, on the current course, it
will happen in Ohio sooner or later.

Governor Bob Taft has been steadfast in his support of
the death penalty, refusing to follow the lead of other gov-
ernors in at least calling for a moratorium on executions
until we can make sure we're putting the right people to
death. Taft's spokesperson insisted, "Ohio has safeguards in
place" to prevent the execution of an innocent man.

Taft speaks with a certainty rarely professed by mortals.
The Greeks called it hubris, the downfall of many of their
heroes. The governor sounds as confident as the Pope, who
is absolutely infallible when he speaks in his official capacity as pastor and teacher. Of course, the Pope is strongly

opposed to the death penalty.

I'm not a religious person, but I think the Bible may be onto something when it says, "Thou shalt not kill." Surely, this is a universal moral imperative if ever there was one. Can we of many faiths not agree: Killing is wrong, no matter who's doing the killing, and no matter who's being killed.

Even if every man sitting on Death Row is guilty of the murder for which he was convicted, that does not justify further murder—even at the hands of the state.

"I'm not one who's saying they're innocent," said Rex Zent, a former prison warden who now runs a support group for ex-inmates. "My guess and my thinking is that's God's decision. And we're playing God with those lives."

Or, as Archbishop Renato Martino said, reiterating to the United Nations the Catholic Church's opposition to death penalty, "The right to life is an inalienable right of every human person."

Sounds like the archbishop took a page out of American history—the page American politicians in favor of the death penalty would rather forget.

The American Dream promised by the Declaration of Independence and the Constitution—equality, justice, and the social harmony we expect would result—remains elusive. But it's still a noble goal, an admirable destination toward which we should strive. The next step on that journey is the abolition of the fundamentally unequal and unjust death penalty.

June 2003

Electrocutions
And Politics

Both Randall Dana, the Ohio Public Defender, and John Quigley, an Ohio State University law professor, charge that Governor George Voinovich, Attorney General Lee Fisher and Common Pleas Judge Richard Sheward are willing to kill people and violate the Ohio Constitution for political gain.

"I think that it's just pure politics, nothing more," Dana said of the lawsuit initiated by Voinovich, filed by Fisher and decided by Sheward.

Judge Sheward recently ruled that the "commutations" granted to seven Death Row defendants by then-Governor Richard Celeste on January 10 and 11, 1991, "are null and void."

When asked how Sheward arrived at his decision, Professor Quigley replied: "By being stupid."

"There's no basis under the Ohio Constitution for the legislature to restrict the governor's power of commutation—any schoolchild could figure it out," Quigley asserts.

The section of the Ohio Constitution reads as follows: "He [the governor] shall have power, after conviction, to grant reprieves, commutations and pardons, for all crimes and offenses except treason and cases of impeachment, upon such conditions as he may think proper; subject, however to such regulations as to the manner of applying for pardons as may be prescribed by law."

"Reprieves and commutations are much less serious things, pardons, however, absolve the person," explained Quigley. "It's an obvious misreading of the constitution," Quigley insists, "to say, like Fisher and Sheward, that *commutations* and *pardons* mean the same thing."

A close reading of the 12-page decision reveals that Sheward arrived at his conclusion by arguing that since the terms *pardon*, *commutation* and *reprieve* are not "mutually exclusive," then they may be used "interchangeably."

John Shoemaker, longtime chief of Ohio's Adult Parole Authority, testified that pardons and commutations were not interchangeable but "are really two different things." Shoemaker defined *commutation* as a reduction of sentence from a higher sentence to a lower, and *pardon* as a forgiveness of a crime.

When asked about Sheward's opinion concerning the "interchangeable" use of the words pardon and commutation, Dana declared, "Well, I think that it's crazy—they obviously mean different things."

"We're living in a very dangerous country. The forces of law and order and the fear of our citizens is reducing the Bill of Rights and Constitution to meaningless documents. Judges are willing to ignore the law and legislatures are willing to pass draconian bills," Dana continued.

Quigley notes, "The governor came in on a pro-death penalty platform as did the attorney general; they think this will be popular."

After the Sheward decision, the *Columbus Dispatch*

reported, "Voinovich supports the death penalty and wanted the commutations reversed."

According to court documents, Voinovich claimed credit for initiating the lawsuit: "The first such contacts were initiated by me when I directed the attorney general to investigate the lawfulness of the clemency."

Voinovich's claim aside, the issue of Fisher's very active participation troubles many Ohio progressives.

In an official statement, Fisher said, "I have never disputed the governor's power to make final clemency determinations, but I have argued under the law that this decision should be made in the light of day in such a way that the rights of the community and the victim are weighed along with those of the prisoner."

Quigley, Dana and co-counsel on the case Adele Shank all complained that the judge's decision to exclude all the Death Row defendants from the trial excluded their side of the story.

"Fisher is being obviously political too," Quigley claimed. "If he was acting ethically he would have told the governor there was no case and would have refused to file it."

Whatever the case, American politicians know that the vast majority of voters favor the death penalty. This puts the United States at odds with the rest of the democratic world.

Since 1957 the United Nations has urged the eradication of capital punishment. Virtually all Western industrial democracies have moved to abolish the death penalty. In countries like Sweden, Finland, Denmark and Portugal, capital punishment was eliminated decades ago. Britain abolished the death penalty in 1965, Canada in 1976 and France in 1981.

In April 1989, Amnesty International appealed to 100 countries, specifically citing the United States and Iran, to abolish the death penalty. The U.S. remains one of only six countries in the world that executes juveniles under age 18, and perhaps the only country officially on record allowing the execution of mentally retarded juveniles as decided in a recent Supreme Court decision.

Amnesty International charged that the death penalty in the United States is applied in an inherently arbitrary and discriminatory manner. The organization noted in its report that while blacks are 12 percent of the population, they account for 40 percent of all Death Row prisoners.

Dana argues that "the amazing factor is that Ohio's Death Row is the most racist in the entire United States. Pennsylvania is a close second."

A state Public Defender's report dated December 1991 indicated that of the 96 inmates on Ohio's Death Row, 51 percent were black, and more than half of the black inmates were convicted of killing a white victim. There was only one case of a white on Death Row for killing a black.

Since executions were resumed in the United States in 1977, 42 of the first 153 people executed were blacks who killed whites. Execution number 154 was so rare it made the following headline in the *New York Times*' September 7, 1991, edition: "White Dies for Killing Black, For The First Time in Decades." The *Times* reported that while more than 90 percent of murders in the United States are intraracial—that is, same race killings—the death penalty disproportionately goes to blacks who kill whites.

Rick Halperin noted in an August 1991 commentary that "the last 12 blacks executed in Louisiana were convicted by all-white juries." This practice was not even allowed in apartheid South Africa.

Shank, also with the Ohio Public Defender's office, said, "We have many more people of African-American decent reflected in our Death Row population. It is over 50 percent on Death Row. And, at the same time Governor Celeste granted these clemencies, all four women on Death Row were African-Americans."

"The death penalty is a racist penalty," said Dana. "There's no two ways about it: It is aimed at poor people, it is aimed at black people. It is just a fact."

Shank concurs that social class is an equally important factor. "I know of only one person on Death Row who had the money to pay for an attorney. Everyone else was indigent and got a court provided attorney." She concluded, "Class was definitely a factor."

"Most of the people come from situations that are not typical middle-class environments, many of them have emotional problems, many of them were abused as children, some of them are suffering from mental disabilities and mental disorders," Shank said.

In his recent book, *Presumed Guilty,* author Martin Yant cites studies that indicate between a one- and three-percent error factor in Death Row convictions.

Shank claims that she is "personally familiar" with six people who had "absolutely nothing to do with the crime" that put them on Death Row. There are others, she argues, who are "not guilty of the level of crime of which they are convicted."

Quigley questions the governor's and attorney general's use of time and resources. "They're spending millions of dollars trying to kill these people."

The *Wall Street Journal* reported in 1986, for example, that the average cost of a death penalty conviction in California was $1.8 million and noted that "the abolition of the death penalty in California would save the taxpayers $125 million a year."

Ironically, virtually none of the money, as Stephen Chapman pointed out in the *Oakland Tribune* in 1991, goes to the defendant. "At least six states limit payment to court-appointed defenders to $1,500 in capital cases... the result is that only the worst lawyers will take on these life-and-death cases and then they lack the funds to do the job right."

Other arguments against the death penalty abound. John Cole Vodicka, who works for the Office for Prisoner and Community Justice of the Oakland Catholic Charities, argues that "state-sanctioned executions expose more of the violence and injustice that are in us all. It is a dehumanizing ritual."

Louise Joylon West, a noted psychiatrist, writes, "That the death penalty is a failure as a deterrent to murder has been demonstrated in many ways. That it is a success as an incentive for murder...is increasingly clear."

In 1981, Michael Kroll offered the following testimony before the U.S. Senate Judiciary Committee: "The truly psychotic in this society—the John Wayne Gacys, the Richard Specks, the Sons of Sam, the Charles Mansons—those people whose behavior is so outside of our comprehension that they have to be seen as aberrant. Not only are such persons not deterred by capital punishment but may in fact flock around it like moths around a flame."

Kroll concluded, "The death penalty actually increases the potential of murder in this country."

Vincent McGee testified at the same hearing and stated, "There are many cases which have been documented of people...who have death wishes, who have a suicidal tendency, but they do not want to kill themselves; they prefer to go out and kill someone else and even demand the death penalty."

The *Louisville Courier-Journal* reported on October 19, 1991, the following story: "Teen Killed Friend Hoping For Execution, Affidavit Says." Indiana State Police Detective Doyle Cornwell swore in an affidavit that Lemuel E. Hickman, 15, told him, "He had attempted suicide several times but was too 'chicken' to go through with it. He [Hickman] thought if he did something 'really bad,' the court would send him to electric chair and 'that'd be it.'"

Governor Voinovich did not personally show up in Sheward's court to address these and other questions concerning Ohio's use of the death penalty. Instead, court records reflect that the governor claimed "executive privilege" and objected to most of the Death Row defendants' written interrogatories.

Quigley stated, "Sheward let him get away with it—it is extremely unusual for anyone who brings a suit to be granted a privilege in order to avoid giving information on the lawsuit they are initiating. It is a weird situation."

Perhaps even stranger is Voinovich's attempt to reconcile his ardent, at least publicly, Catholicism with his actions in this case. Voinovich has long cited his Catholicism in conjunction with his anti-abortion stance. Yet the Catholic bishops are on record since 1980 with a statement that reads in part: "We believe that abolition of the death penalty is most consonant with the example of Jesus, who both taught and practiced the forgiveness of injustice... there is and has been a certain sense that even in those cases where serious justifications can be offered for the necessity of taking life, those who are identified in a special way with Christ should refrain from taking life."

Dana, a self-described Goldwater Republican, offered this observation: "Never trust a liberal, they will sell you out in a minute. Lee Fisher has sold out his constituency when be brought these lawsuits. He was looking at possibly having to run again for election. He sold his soul on the issue of the death penalty because he wanted his job. Seven people may die because of Lee Fisher's political ambition."

David Bruck concluded his 1983 article in *The New Republic*, "Decision of Death," with this: "The day when Americans stop condemning people to death on the basis of race and inequality will be the day when we stop condemning anyone to death at all."

Columbus Free Press
March 1992

Justice Denied

In the very near future, an innocent person is likely to die in Ohio's electric chair. The *Columbus Free Press* has uncovered new evidence that substantially confirms the alarming allegations that indigent defendants—including many on Death Row—were denied due process.

A recent complaint filed in the Franklin County Common Pleas Court supports earlier allegations made by Chester "Briss" Craig, former deputy investigator at the Ohio Public Defender's Office (OPDO), that Richard Smith, a former public defender investigator, falsified records and failed to investigate cases of Death Row inmates, especially those that involved blacks. When viewed with a recently completed State Highway Patrol report by Trooper Marc Rogols, the Ohio Public Defender's Office may have engaged in perhaps one of the most shocking scandals in state history.

Linda Leisure, who runs a Death Row ministry, sent a letter dated October 25, 1994, to Judge James J. O'Grady. She alleged that "Mr. Smith called me after this case was settled and wanted me to inflate the bill I was sending to the court. I refused to go along with this and at this point disassociated myself permanently from Mr. Smith and Fox Investigations."

Leisure was assisting Smith and his Fox Investigation

Company in the case of *State of Ohio v. Brian Eugene Long*. Leisure told the *Free Press* that Smith "wanted me to falsify time reports and interviews on these murder cases."

On November 14, 1994, Leisure voluntarily underwent a polygraph examination. A copy of the exam reads:

"Did Richard Smith ask you to inflate your mitigation bill on the Brian E. Long Case?"

"Yes."

"Did Mr. Smith ask you to alter summaries on the Brian E. Long case?"

"Yes."

Polygraph examiner M.D. Ketter concluded, "No deception indicated."

In January 1992, Craig had written a complaint to the Ohio Investigator General that charged: "Some of our investigators previously assigned to Ohio Public Defender's clients before they were convicted had not met with or conducted any kind of investigation on behalf of these clients... Many of these clients, mostly black, indicated they had never heard the name of the investigator mentioned and that they had never met with such person. Such information led me to believe that some of the investigators were turning in false time reports and were not providing the support services to the attorneys as required."

These are shocking allegations, supported now by new evidence, against the then-investigators at the OPDO—a state agency charged with providing legal representation for poor people throughout the state of Ohio. Craig claimed that during Smith's tenure at the OPDO from April 1983 to November 1988, Smith referred to black indigent defendants as "niggers" and white defendants as "scumbags." These "niggers" and "scumbags" were the very clients that Smith was working for, investigating their claims of innocence and ensuring justice.

Craig told the *Free Press* that both Smith and another investigator, Patricia Cyrus, "spent weeks on trial-level cases [but] not conducting interviews with mostly black clients." Craig explained how his original allegations came about. "We did what we call a post conviction and we go talk to jurors and find out what we did wrong, and we also go back and talk to witnesses that we had, and there's several cases where we talked to witnesses and said, 'That's not what you told Dick Smith or Pat Cyrus when they interviewed you.' And they come back and say, 'Who's Dick Smith? Who's Pat Cyrus? I never talked to them.'"

Craig provided the *Free Press* with what appears to be falsified case logs. These same pages were Exhibit 18 in the State Highway Patrol investigation of Craig's original allegations.

The patrol issued a 1,816-page investigation document that contains bizarre revelation after bizarre revelation. The report's findings about employees of the OPDO, besides two widely publicized first-degree misdemeanor convictions for theft in office, include:

• While on investigations, Chief Investigator John O'Connor carried on a long-distance relationship with a female in Findlay, Ohio, and routinely obtained unauthorized police reports from the Findlay police department through a female manager at a Holiday Inn;

• Investigator Gary Blankenship was having an affair with another woman in the Findlay area while on state business;

• William Kitts, OPDO deputy director, was arrested in Reynoldsburg, Ohio, and plead guilty to a DUI with a blood-alcohol content level of 1.33, but he was also charged with three counts of drug abuse, one count of drug paraphernalia and one count of lane straddling that were later dropped and the records have been sealed in this case;

• Attorney Robert Head, who had his license to practice law suspended in the state of Ohio for violation of the professional code of ethics—stealing a ring from an evidence room—was then hired by Randall Dana, the Ohio Public Defender, as a political favor;

• Investigator Jeff Layman was disciplined for the unauthorized use and destruction of a state automobile while out on a weekend date;

• Richard Smith attempted to set up Briss Craig on a drunk-driving charge after a party celebrating Craig's graduation from the Ohio Peace Officer's Training Program.

According to the report, investigators were living it up at the Ritz Carlton, engaging in unauthorized spying on each other and hanging out with serial rapist Billy Milligan and multi-millionaire conman Marvin Warner. Apparently there were no limits to what this wild bunch was willing to do.

This sordid and strange tale of mostly bad ex-cops run amok as even worse state public defender investigators was originally brought to the public's attention courtesy of Briss Craig.

Craig was hired in the state Public Defender's Office in May 1982; he was among the first blacks working in that agency. Craig admits to being a political appointee, through his friendship with then Columbus City Attorney (and later Mayor) Greg Lashuka. ·

Craig claimed his problems began when he was promoted to deputy investigator under John O'Grady. As Richard Lord, Craig's attorney, explains it, "They had an old boy's club. Perhaps had Briss played along, they wouldn't have tried to set him up."

After his promotion, Craig told the investigators that their expense reports and investigative reports were "bullshit" and didn't make sense. Within a few weeks, Richard Smith, an ex-Columbus police officer working under Craig, was promoted to deputy director. Smith purportedly told friends and fellow investigators that he couldn't work under a "nigger," according to several witnesses.

As Craig tells it, "O'Connor had a thing about ex-cops... Oh man, he loved ex-cops. He was a cop wannabe. No background checks were required. So someone like Smith, who was forced off the Columbus police force for exposing himself to young girls in German Village, could step right in and become a deputy investigator."

When Craig questioned the activities of the investigators under him, they would respond, "Do you want to know what I had for breakfast too?" Toward the end of March 1986, Craig wrote a "Do You Want To Know What I Had For Breakfast" memo to David Stebbins, chief of the Death Penalty Litigation Division, outlining the resistance of the investigators to administrative accountability. Stebbins later told the investigators that the OPDO's office was not a "cop shop" and that they needed to knock off some of their more outrageous behaviors.

But OPDO investigators Gary Blankenship and William Buxton allegedly continued to steal from the public treasury by padding their expense accounts and charging expensive stereo equipment to the department and diverting it for their own personal use.

Smith had a more interesting plan, according to the report of Ohio Highway Patrol Trooper Marc Rogols. With the assistance of Cyrus, Smith allegedly plotted to have Craig arrested by the Findlay police for drunk driving after a party at Cyrus' sister's house. Only Blankenship's refusal to go along with Smith foiled the plan.

Blankenship told Rogols that he was "ordered not to drive [Craig] back" by Smith. "He called me outside and he said, 'Gary,' he says, 'let Craig drive back to the Academy.' I said, 'Dick, I can't do that. He's in no condition to drive.' He says, 'Well, I'm ordering you not to drive.' So I looked and I said OK. So when Craig came out…we walked down to the car. I told Craig I'd drive. I walked back down to Dick and said, 'Sorry, I can't do it, too much liability. Somebody could get hurt or killed.'"

Smith offered a different version to Ohio Highway Patrol Trooper Marc Rogols, who investigated the allegations. Smith blamed the set-up on Buxton: "Buxton was going to call one of his friends who worked the night shift over there and have him watch the car, and if Craig was drunk, he was going to take him."

But Judy Kendrick, a friend of Smith, later sent an unsolicited letter to Ohio Public Defender Dana backing Blankenship's story: "I am referring to one scheme instigated by Patty Cyrus and Richard Smith. I did read the investigative report written by your office, so I know you are familiar with the details. It was exactly as Smith confided in me before the incident."

Rogols interviewed Kendrick independently and confirmed her letter. Rogols wrote: "Kendrick also knew of a 'scheme' by Smith to 'set-up' Craig on a DUI charge. The 'set-up' involved Craig's presence at an office party in the

London, Ohio, area. Smith arranged for Craig to 'get drunk' and for a friend on the police department to 'wait for the arrest.' Smith told Kendrick that the 'purpose of this "set-up" was to get Craig fired.'"

Kendrick told Rogols that Smith's actions were racially motivated; Blankenship concurred. Meanwhile, Smith seemingly took to spying on Craig. Smith and Cyrus' surveillance of Craig paid dividends in May 1987. They managed to get Craig suspended for two days for allowing a non-state employee to use his state car.

On September 25, 1988, another investigator, Michael Monk, was hired. According to Craig, Monk fit right in with Smith and Cyrus and immediately learned the "niggers and scumbags" lingo. Monk was allegedly fond of carrying a gun at all times and knew Smith well, since he was dating Smith's daughter. On or about the same time, Smith's daughter was also dating Billy Milligan, according to the highway patrol report.

In September, the set-up plot was uncovered by top administrators at the OPDO. On March 18, 1989, Cyrus ceased employment at the office; Smith left voluntarily on a disability claim on May 8; and Monk left on July 18.

Craig claims that "O'Connor had me remove 'papers' from the [OPDO] office" concerning the cessation of Cyrus, Smith and Monk's employment. He further alleges that "Randall Dana agreed not to fight Richard Smith's disability claim, which he knew or had reason to believe was false, if Mr. Smith would agree to leave his position with the Ohio Public Defender in lieu of being fired for various civil rights violations."

Kendrick supports this allegation in her letter to Dana:

"Now, in comparison, Dick Smith was caught, and he told my husband and I that you said you would 'go along with his claim of disability' if he would come in and resign… Smith confided to me that he hurt his back taking the cover off his hot tub."

Craig later testified under oath that Richard Smith not only falsified reports, but did little or nothing when it came to investigating the claims of black Death Row defendants. He further testified that, in the Sanford murder case, "After a number of investigators had been on this case for weeks and weeks and weeks, and after I had personally asked them to go to interview certain black people that had knowledge of the crime and it was never done… I came to the conclusion…that they were doing nothing." Craig confronted a group of investigators on this matter.

On April 2, 1990, Stebbins reorganized the office, stripping Craig of much of his authority. In July 1990, Craig retained the services of attorney Richard Lord to investigate possible civil rights claims that he might have against the OPDO. Craig sought Lord's counsel not only about being stripped of his various duties and responsibilities, but also complained about racial harassment and specifically Smith's DUI scheme and surveillance.

In November, Craig submitted a written memorandum to Stebbins regarding racially discriminatory practices and serious charges concerning improper use of state funds at the OPDO. Craig says, despite repeated follow-ups, little or no corrective action was taken. In Craig's memo, he alleged that certain employees had submitted fraudulent expense reports and investigative reports and were improperly granted "comp time." A face-to-face meeting on December 11, 1990, with Stebbins yielded nothing, according to Craig.

In April 1991, Craig's duties were further reduced. He felt this was a direct result of his whistle-blowing memo.

On June 25, 1991, the OPDO began an investigation of Craig in response to charges by an inmate, Harold Bolser, and his girlfriend, identified in public records as Ms. Vanderkolt. Both alleged that Craig had agreed to "fix" Bolser's parole through his friendship with people on the parole board. On July 15, 1991, Dana took the unusual step of contracting an outside agency—ironically, the Ohio Highway Patrol—to investigate the bribery charge against Craig. While contesting this charge, Craig took a five-week vacation from July to August 1991.

On September 9, 1991, Robert Lane, a "neutral and detached administrator," found "there's no reasonable basis to find that Mr. Craig agreed to fix Mr. Bolser's parole or that he guaranteed Mr. Bolser's release." Moreover, Lane found that Craig was not guilty of "malfeasance" either.

On a lesser charge, Lane found that Craig did, in fact, "demonstrate a lack of honesty and integrity...with his acceptance of outside employment without written con-sent" of the OPDO. Lane recommended "that Mr. Craig be suspended, without pay, for an appropriate period of time."

On September 11, 1991, Chester "Briss" Craig was ter-minated from the OPDO office. Rumors flew that Craig had been set up in retaliation for his November 1990 whis-tle-blowing memo. According to Craig, one investigator, James Primsner, told Michelle Samuels, another investiga-tor, that Bolser had been part of a plot to get Craig. Craig and Lord report that Samuels told them "that the plan to get rid of Briss" began in 1990, according to Primsner.

In January 1992, Craig sent a list of 33 allegations—virtually all confirmed by the Rogols Report—to the state Inspector General David Sturtz. Sturtz turned the investigation over to the Ohio Highway Patrol. On February 20, Major W.H. Davies, Commander of the Office of Investigative Services for the highway patrol, informed Craig that his allegations were being investigated by Trooper Rogols.

Rogols' thorough investigation established evidence of expense account abuse and falsified public records by state public defender investigators. Rogols' investigation also reported that the destruction and shredding of documents was ongoing during the investigation.

On October 3, 1992, Public Defender Randall Dana resigned, citing "burnout." Virtually all of the top administrators of the OPDO followed suit.

Rogols concluded his investigation on July 19, 1994. Two former public defenders—Blankenship and Buxton—pleaded guilty to first-degree misdemeanor theft charges. Rogols notes: "The Franklin County Prosecutor's Office recommended against prosecuting any of the other principals included in the allegations, as did the Hancock County Prosecutor concerning the computerized criminal history information that allegedly involved the Findlay Police Department."

Nevertheless, Rogols' investigative report stands as a lasting testament to the monumental injustices perpetrated by the investigators at the Ohio Public Defender's Office. They betrayed the trust of indigent clients—"niggers" and "scumbags" in the investigator's eyes. Now evidence suggests that there are possibly innocent people, and certainly over-charged people, awaiting death in

Ohio penitentiaries because of the gross misconduct of public officials.

The *Free Press* handed Craig a list of Death Row defendants and asked him to check the names of those he felt were denied due process because of falsified reports. He quickly checked the names of 15 Death Row inmates:

- Anthony C. Apanovitch
- Michael Bueke
- Robert Buell
- John William Byrd
- Gregory Esparza
- Jeff Lundgren
- Ernest Martin
- Alfred J. Morales
- Rhett De Pew
- Martin Rojas
- Billie Joe Sowell
- David Steffen
- William Wickline Jr.
- Donald Williams
- William G. Zuern

The *Free Press* calls for a federal investigation regarding the shocking and scandalous revelations in the Rogols Report before the politically expedient and irrevocable execution of some innocent man.

Columbus Free Press
January 1995

Ashes To Ashes, Dust To Dust

Yes, Columbus' trash-burning power plant has shut down, thanks to the U.S. EPA, plant whistle-blowers and environmental activists. We all learned the dangers of deadly dioxin and the community is safer for it. But what of the fate of those who worked inside the plant?

Now, courageous workers have come forward to document the atrocities that happened during the 11 years the plant operated—and how employees and work-release prisoners were poisoned there.

In the Vietnam era, more than a few local hoods were given the choice: 'Nam or prison. In a new variation on the old theme, men sentenced in Franklin County were given the option: work in toxic ash or go to jail.

The ash they labored in was loaded with contaminants: lead, cadmium, arsenic and, for old time's sake, dioxins—arguably the deadliest chemical on the planet and the active ingredient in Agent Orange. You remember Agent Orange, don't you—it will kill a tropical rainforest overnight, but won't harm humans? Right!

In the new scam, "sentenced residents" hand-picked metals, often without gloves, from the trash plant's toxic ash heaps in a practice so shockingly unsafe it gives literal

20

meaning to the old adage "ashes to ashes, dust to dust."

Despite a denial from Paul Weick, president of Shaneway—the private company sifting the ash—eyewitnesses confirm earlier reports in the *Columbus Free Press* and the *Columbus Guardian* that the company was running an unsafe "mining operation" at Columbus' trash-burning power plant using sentenced work-released laborers.

"They were separating metal from the ash stream. They would stand over top of the ash and literally pull the metals from the toxic ash and they'd have to keep the machinery running," said Michael Dray, a former stationary engineer at the plant. "The whole installation was put in over five years ago. It really is technically a mining operation, extracting metals from the waste stream."

Randy Pepper, a former crane operator, said the Shaneway laborers had "the dirtiest job there was." He said the ash belt operators "would come out black," and that he saw the Shaneway workers "all the time, they didn't wear respirators and they were working right in it."

The "prisoners"—excuse me, "residents"—were reportedly paid around $5 an hour, according to a resident supervisor. You see, prisoners who make license plates usually don't get paid—at least not minimum wage—but sentenced residents do. The Jackson Pike jail facility functions like a giant halfway house.

The treatment of the so-called "work-release residents" was often far more dangerous than the employees of the trash-burning power plant. These often two-time offenders for non-violent crimes—given a last chance to work or do hard time in the county jail or the state penitentiary—may have had their lucky break turn into a lingering unintended, unbeknownst death row sentence. "Cancer, you say.

Wonder how I got that?" They had the misfortune of being housed in the Jackson Pike facility right across the street from the largest known source of deadly dioxin in the United States, at a time the plant needed surplus fodder—I mean, labor.

Recently obtained internal memos from the plant document that employees at the trash-burner exposed to the ash suffered toxic levels of lead, cadmium, arsenic and dioxin. An affidavit from William Murphy, former safety manager at the plant, affirms that, despite his repeated warnings to Plant Manager John Heiger, employees at the plant were exposed to arsenic levels 2.5 times those allowed by OSHA standards; cadmium levels at five times; lead at 138 times; and dioxin at levels 770 times the ambient air in the community.

The *Free Press* has obtained a signed statement from a resident supervisor at the Jackson Pike facility claiming many of the sentenced residents who worked for Shaneway "were covered with ash and had visible skin problems" consistent with the symptoms of chloroacne caused by dioxin exposure. When asked how many showed signs of skin condition, the supervisor replied, "All of them."

All the residents supervised by our source worked in the ash collection unit south of the main complex, where Shaneway contracted to extract non-ferrous metals from the toxic ash.

Steve Cahill, now the assistant chief of probation for Franklin County, then the director of work-release, acknowledges that Shaneway was a subcontractor to the Solid Waste Authority of Central Ohio (SWACO) and "a frequent employer of work-release residents." Cahill said that "announcements over the loudspeaker" were made at the Jackson Pike facility for Shaneway interviews.

Some resident supervisors suggest that more residents than usual were taken into the facility because of the easy availability of jobs at Shaneway.

Cahill claimed that he "never received a complaint from a resident" and that he was "unaware" of any safety hazards. Moreover, he contended that if there were hazards, "It would have been SWACO's and Shaneway's responsibility to inform him." His brother, Jeffrey M. Cahill, is on the board of trustees of SWACO and also works for the health department.

Steve Cahill noted that he "never received any correspondence from either SWACO or Shaneway" regarding danger to the residents. He conceded that whatever they were doing over there was "a dirty job." Cahill guessed that the residents had worked for Shaneway since 1989. Cahill admitted that "a lot of employees were sick at the work-release center, some from cancer," and that he had filed a letter with OSHA to investigate health conditions at the center. One of his employees had a "rare form of lymph cancer" and another had died of thyroid cancer. The oldest cancer victim was in his fifties.

Gail Dittmer, current director of work-release, said, "We didn't have any medical complaints. Whether they saw their own doctor, if so, they didn't report it." She also conceded the work was "dirty." She said, "We had some people who didn't want to work there because of the dirty work."

Robin Rutan, the facility's case manager for Shaneway's work-release residents, stressed that "it was convenience since they were right across the street from the Jackson

Pike facility." The residents' job, as Rutan understood it, "was to sort through stuff that was brought in." She noted that it was "a pretty dirty job" and that the workers were "sometimes covered" in ash.

A resident supervisor—who remains anonymous for fear of job loss—and two former residents tell a different story. It was the supervisor's job to "pat down" the residents after they returned from work. "They were literally covered in ash with no protective clothing or equipment," the source insisted.

Michael Dray confirmed this. He remembered one of the residents "coming off a night shift and bumming a cigarette from me, and he was just covered with ash from head to toe."

The supervisor mentioned above said he "personally drove residents back to jail who refused to work" in the toxic ash. Many complained about headaches and problems with breathing. The *Free Press* has also learned that one resident was taken to the emergency room at Grant Hospital with breathing problems.

Both Rutan and Dittmer deny that any workers were returned to jail for refusing to work for Shaneway. "If there were some disciplinary problems, then they would be sent to jail. They weren't sent because they quit," Dittmer offered.

Much like the homeless who were used in San Francisco to remove asbestos without safety equipment, and like the well-documented nomadic crews of illegal immigrants that are used by the pollution industry, residents are a perfect marginalized, transient population for toxic labor. As Dittmer explained, "Some worked there for up to six months; the majority had shorter sentences. But, there's no way we can go back and find every person who worked over there."

SWACO and Shaneway may have been knowingly violating federal and state occupational safety and health laws. William Murphy says that residents worked at the trash plant "in all capacities." But he was shocked to hear what the subcontractor, Shaneway, was doing: "I can't believe they would let people crawl around in that stuff. There's going to be long-term health consequences."

A memo dated April 6, 1993, from Murphy to Robert R. Santa, customer service coordinator, advised, "I believe that it would be prudent of you to demand the same level of safety for a contractor's employees as we provide for our employees. If we do not, negligence could become an issue if an accident occurs involving a contractor's employee. Persons working in the same environment must be provided the same protection."

Murphy pointed out that under law, "We have a responsibility to protect all workers, even frequenters. I told John Heiger we had a serious problem with the ash and arsenic after tests came back from Ross Labs."

One of SWACO's employees, Teddy Hodge, tested at "an extremely high level of arsenic," and Dick Reese, an employee in the safety department, also "had high levels." "That plant was a very scary place to work. You never knew what the arsenic, cadmium, lead or dioxin levels were," the former safety director confessed.

Paul Weick vehemently denies any allegations that his company's employees were put at risk: "This is an absolute lie." He denies that he's ever seen any workers in regular clothes covered with ash, but does point out that many workers had "their own work clothes."

"I don't know that we provided them with clothes or it was necessary," Weick insisted.

Murphy disagrees and points out that the OSHA laws are quite clear on toxic contaminants: The uniforms must remain on location and workers must shower before leaving the premises.

"We've done everything we can to protect our workers and have done so over the years—these are unfounded allegations. I'm disturbed someone is coming after us," huffed Weick.

And victory is right around the corner in Vietnam—there's light at the end of the ash tunnel.

Columbus Free Press
June 1995

Dirty Little Secrets

The death penalty is primarily political. It's about power: Who gets killed, and who gets elected prosecutor, judge, attorney general and governor.

You may recall our own Dewey Stokes, Franklin County Commissioner, ran pro-death penalty commercials during his last campaign, although the issue is totally unrelated to his office. No doubt Dewey wants to fry all the Hueys and Louies on Death Row, but what about Attorney General Betty "The Great Expediter" Montgomery? Betty wants to hide "the dirty little secrets" of Ohio's Death Row by speeding up executions.

Those of us who are more concerned with justice than expediency, or Ms. Montgomery's political future, need to shed some light on her secrets:

Secret #1: Tony Apanovitch, a small time crook, stands convicted of rape and murder based on circumstantial evidence. Apanovitch is a top priority of the Central Ohio Amnesty International organization. The prosecution withheld crucial evidence that surely would have caused a jury to conclude that there was "reasonable doubt."

For example, Apanovitch voluntarily supplied hair, blood and saliva samples to the police. Police investigators recorded that the samples were "not consistent" with the killer. A hair found on the victim did not match hers or Apanovitch's. But the hair was consistent with that from a serial rapist that had attacked and brutalized six women in the same neighborhood.

Also, police investigators confirmed Apanovitch's alibi of his whereabouts the night of the murder, but failed as required under law to inform Apanovitch's lawyer. Moreover, the prosecutor, eager for a win, misinformed the jury about the odds of Apanovitch's semen—type A—being found in the victim. It seems the prosecutor failed to mention that the victim was also a "type A" secretor, making the evidence meaningless.

Apanovitch has been on Death Row for 12 years, and is seeking a new trial that would undoubtedly free him.

Secret #2: John G. Spirko Jr. was convicted on circumstantial evidence of murdering Elgin, Ohio's postmaster Betty Jean Mottinger. Unlike the O.J. Simpson case, there was no physical evidence linking Spirko to the death scene.

Former Ohio Public Defender Randall Dana stated that public defenders were "convinced that, for whatever reason, the Postal Department had set about proving this guy did it—Spirko did it—when in fact, someone else was guilty."

Former investigator Chester "Briss" Craig produced a notarized affidavit dated March 17, 1988, from William Green, a prisoner in the Marion Correctional Institution, swearing that his cellmate, John Willier, confessed in great detail to the killing of Betty Mottinger. Green's affidavit reads: "When John Willier related this aforesaid account of the kidnapping and killing of the post mistress to me, he was crying and appeared to be in an emotionally overwrought state."

Spirko was scheduled to die on January 5, 1995, but received a stay of execution and his case has since been picked up "pro bono" by a prominent Washington, D.C., law firm.

Secret #3: There may be at least 14 other Apanovitchs and Spirkos on Ohio's Death Row. In January 1992, Chester Craig filed a formal complaint with the Ohio Inspector General that reads, "Some of our investigators previously assigned to Ohio Public Defender's clients before they were convicted had not met with or conducted any kind of investigation on behalf of these clients."

Craig has personally identified to me the names of the following Death Row inmates who may not have received due process as required by the U.S. Constitution: David Steffen, Ernest Martin, John William Byrd, Michael Bueke, Billie Joe Sowell, Robert Buell, Gregory Esparza, Donald Williams, William A. Zuern, Rhett de Pew, William Wickline Jr., Alfred J. Morales, Martin Rojas and Jeff Lundgren.

Craig claimed, "Many of these clients, mostly black, indicated they had never heard the name of the investigator mentioned and that they had never met with such person." Craig concluded that investigators for the Public Defender's Office, where he was a supervisor, "were turning in false time reports and were not providing the support services to the attorneys as required."

A 1994 report by the Office of Investigative Services substantially supports Craig's allegations. Additionally, Linda Leisure, who worked for one of the investigators, told the *Columbus Free Press* in January 1995 that she was asked "to falsify time reports and interviews on these murder cases."

Unlike O.J., who with six lawyers and millions of dollars won acquittal, or the Menendez brothers, whose vast fortune allowed them to skirt the death penalty despite their confessions, Apanovitch and the others cannot afford simple justice under our system. They can't buy a Dream Team of lawyers, expert witnesses and top-notch investigators.

If O.J. were poor, the only thing an Ohio prosecutor would've had to say to a jury is: "This is undeniably the hair of a black man in this glove." Guilty as charged. And he would've gotten the death penalty for killing an upper-class white woman. If his victim had been another poor black man, maybe he would have gotten four years in prison.

That's why we need to go slow, despite Betty's political ambitions. If she had her way, both Apanovitch and Spirko would be dead by now.

April 24, 1996

Prison Stripes
To Pinstripes

As the costs continue to mount from the Easter 1993 Lucasville riot, some are starting to complain that not all the bad guys were wearing prison stripes—a few may have been in pinstripe suits.

As a special prosecutor for the trials of George Skatzes and Jason Robb, both Lucasville inmates convicted of aggravated murder in the slaying of Corrections Officer Robert Vallandingham during the riot, Dan Hogan convinced two juries to sentence the men to death. These career-building cases paid off handsomely for Hogan. He earned nearly $100,000 in extra income while at the same time working full-time as an assistant Franklin County Prosecutor.

Hogan's success in holding down the two jobs no doubt aided his election a year later to the position of Franklin County Common Pleas judge. Now, he's having a harder time convincing his colleagues at the courthouse that he wasn't "double-dipping." Court insiders are questioning the system that allowed Hogan to keep his full-time job as county prosecutor while more than doubling his yearly salary in 1995 with his second high-profile job.

An April 1997 *Columbus Dispatch* article itemized the

"Costly prosecutions"—state expenses associated with the Lucasville riots—including the two death penalty cases Hogan prosecuted. Conspicuously missing in the *Dispatch* itemization was the amount of Hogan's salary. In the Skatzes and Robb cases, the *Dispatch* provided the amounts paid to defense attorneys, jury members, expert witnesses, private investigators and judges, but not prosecutors. Hogan, endorsed by the Republican party, was also endorsed by the *Dispatch* in his 1996 non-partisan campaign against Beverly Farlow for judge.

Records from Lynn Alan Grimshaw, Scioto County prosecuting attorney, show that Hogan billed $99,240 in 13 non-consecutive monthly invoices between September 1994 and January 1996 for his work as a Lucasville special prosecutor. By subtracting the August 1995 invoice, when Hogan billed only 2.25 hours and was paid $135, a 12-month or the yearly equivalent of Hogan's salary was $99,105 for working 1,652 hours. A typical work year is 2,080 hours.

At the same time, Franklin County Auditor records indicate that Hogan earned $61,300 as a Franklin County Prosecutor in 1994 in addition to the $21,255 he made in four months for the Lucasville cases. In 1995, Hogan's salary dropped by a third to $41,777 while his Lucasville earnings increased by three-and-a-half times to $73,725. By working simultaneously for Franklin County and as a Lucasville special prosecutor, his yearly salary in '95 was $115,552.

Columbus Alive interviewed various judges, prosecutors and court officials about the practice—none who were critical of Judge Hogan would speak on the record—but they were very blunt when anonymity was assured. Court insiders complain that Hogan essentially held two jobs and was "double-dipping." As one put it, "Look, everybody knows that he should've taken a leave of absence and not worked at all [as a county prosecutor] during the trial. But nobody wanted to question the prosecutor trying to put the rioters on Death Row."

Another claims that Franklin County judges made inquiries to the prosecutor's office when Hogan and fellow prosecutor Doug Stead failed to appear when scheduled for local criminal cases. "We were told that Hogan was working 'off the record.' That means every time a state trooper or FBI investigator [in regards to the Lucasville trials] called him in his office, he had to log out as a Franklin County Prosecutor and log in as a Lucasville prosecutor. We all laughed," one said.

"There were times when they [Stead and Hogan] were supposed to be at the Lucasville trial when they were at the Franklin County Courthouse and times when they were supposed to be in Franklin County when they were working in Lucasville. It was a logistical nightmare, but I'm sure Dan kept detailed records," one prosecutor said.

One skeptical Hogan-watcher said, "Give me a break. He's got hundreds of calls from troopers and investigators. How in the hell is he going to check in and out and not double-dip? There's an easy way to answer this question. Ask the state police for their contact logs and discussions with Hogan concerning witnesses. Not what the witnesses said; they can list them A to Z, and see whether they match up with Hogan's daily logs."

Retired Assistant State Auditor Henry J. Schutte examined Hogan's payroll records at *Alive's* request. "There's some obvious red flags that I would have looked at when I was an auditor," Schutte noted.

Schutte pointed out that in December 1994, during the holiday season, Hogan billed a combined total of 343 hours, or 11 hours a day for 31 straight days. The next December he billed a combined 412 hours that averaged out to over 13.25 hours a day for 31 straight days.

"If he's claiming 412 hours in a month, he'd better be putting in 412 hours and documenting it, or it's possible theft in office because tax money's involved," Schutte said. "And he can't be doing Lucasville work on Franklin County time."

Doug Stead, a senior Franklin County Prosecutor and also a Lucasville special prosecutor, billed 327.5 hours in December 1994, costing taxpayers $19,650. While Stead was included in the December 1994 payroll reports from Grimshaw, he was absent from the remaining 12 billings despite public accounts of payment. Thus, *Alive* was not able to track his monthly totals.

In February 1995, as Hogan put in over 312 hours at a cost of $18,735 on the Robb case, he still managed to bill Franklin County for 19 hours, averaging 12-hour billable days. Many question the effectiveness of one person working so many hours on two jobs.

Hogan could not be reached for comment, although he and *Alive* exchanged several phone messages.

Riot negotiator Niki Schwartz, a Cleveland attorney, credited Robb with helping end the riots. Schwartz testified that, "Jason deserves a large portion of the credit for the peaceful resolution of the riot.... I have substantial doubts about his guilt."

He was adamant in his testimony that Robb and Skatzes were not getting "fair trials." Robb steadfastly denied that he wanted guard Robert Vallandingham killed. "I knew Bobby Vallandingham. I liked Bobby, we had respect for each other," Robb said.

Schwartz pointed out that Hogan and other prosecutors were being paid more than defense attorneys and had an unfair advantage since they "had the use of the state highway patrol's computerized files," according to the *Dispatch*.

Another aspect of the riot usually ignored is the documented inhumane conditions at Lucasville in the five years prior to the prisoner uprising. In June 1988, Lucasville inmates filed a human rights complaint with Amnesty International providing detailed accounts of prisoner abuses. Prisoners were kept for up to 11 straight years in "J1 Supermax" cells, constantly monitored and deprived of fresh air and sunshine. Prisoners alleged that sadistic beatings occurred regularly, sometimes resulting in deaths. The use of fire hoses was common.

So deplorable were the conditions at Lucasville that human rights activists worldwide monitored the facility. Dennis Brown of the University of Edinburgh wrote a Lucasville inmate in November 1989: "I was shocked and saddened to read in the newspaper here of your situation and the conditions under which you are being contained. How can a country which claims to uphold life and liberty treat its citizens as you are being treated? ... Because of the dreadful way you have and are being treated, the world is learning about Ohio penal industries and the American penal system. The injustices inflicted on you are bringing international shame on your country."

The conditions were so bad that the usually conservative Correctional Institution Inspection Committee (CIIC) called for a full-scale investigation in 1990. Then-

Governor Richard Celeste ordered an investigation by the state Highway Patrol as well, after the CIIC and the FBI looked into allegations that two black prisoners were killed by white guards after touching a white nurse.

The *Dispatch* recently reported that the 11-day riot, leaving 10 persons dead at Lucasville, cost the state nearly $70 million. Years of whitewashing and overlooking prisoner complaints at Lucasville inevitably led to the Easter riot, tragic loss of life and soaring financial costs to the taxpayers. It remains to be seen whether the behavior of those in pinstripes will be scrutinized as carefully as those in prison stripes.

July 14, 1997

Political Prisoner

An outspoken critic of the Ohio prison system has taken his case to the state's highest court. This week, attorneys for Native American activist and fugitive Timothy "Little Rock" Reed petitioned the Ohio Supreme Court for a writ of habeas corpus. They asked the court to "order [Reed's] immediate release and discharge from parole" or "conduct a hearing or appoint a 'neutral and detached' hearing officer to determine if [he] should be immediately released and discharged from parole."

Reed, a former inmate at Ohio's Lucasville prison, was on parole just prior to the well-known 1993 Easter riot. A frequent critic of prison officials' practices at Lucasville, Reed had warned repeatedly in writing of the possibility of a riot at the prison.

He was cited for parole violations and faced likely re-incarceration at the prison when, with only six weeks remaining on his parole, he fled Ohio in early 1993. Reed claimed he feared retaliation for criticizing Ohio prison policy. He later spent an additional four months and one week in a New Mexico jail awaiting extradition to Ohio after being arrested in September 1994. Reed fought the extradition to the New Mexico Supreme Court. In September 1997, in a 4-1 decision, Reed convinced that court that his fears were justified.

The state of New Mexico refused to return Reed to Ohio for parole violations, saying authorities could not protect Reed from injury or death at the hands of prison officials or other inmates should he be re-incarcerated. Forty-one state attorney generals took the position that the New Mexico court's refusal to extradite Reed undid 100 years of interstate extradition practice. The U.S. Supreme Court later reversed the New Mexico Supreme Court's decision and ordered his extradition to Ohio.

In their petition, attorneys C. Matthew Cooper and Cary Rodman Cooper argued that "it is unlawful for state authorities to deprive a parolee of liberty in retaliation for the parolee's protected speech activities." The Coopers asserted, among other claims, that "state parole and prison officials...have a history of retaliating against [Reed]" because of his free speech activities.

They also claimed that Reed was "justified in fleeing custody" since fleeing was his only "reasonable choice...to protect himself from immediate threat of great bodily harm or death."

Reed's attorneys submitted an affidavit from Steve J. Martin, the former chief of staff of the Texas Department of Corrections, who has investigated major prison disturbances in Texas, California, New York, Ohio and Puerto Rico. Martin studied the Lucasville riot and issued a report in a February 1996 civil suit listing 12 primary causes of the Lucasville riot, such as:

• "Inadequate intelligence system on inmate gang activity"

• "Interracial double celling"

• "Lack of adequate security supervision of Muslim religious group prior to riot"

Reed complained in a July 1991 letter to Lucasville Warden Arthur Tate Jr. that "Your practice of forcing racially integrated celling of prisoners is directly contrary to your stated intentions of making this prison safer." Reed asked Tate, "Do you want a riot, or just a few 'isolated incidents'?"

Martin called Lucasville "a troubled facility long before the April riot erupted." "The warden of Lucasville knew that the problems existed," he wrote. Martin believes that if Reed had been re-incarcerated in Lucasville, "that a reasonable person in Mr. Reed's position would have had ample reason to fear for his safety."

A state report on the Lucasville riot authored by Columbus Safety Director Thomas Rice, then in charge of the Ohio Highway Patrol, noted the presence of the Aryan Brotherhood at Lucasville; even certain guards wore the distinct "SS" lightning-bolt tattoos associated with the neo-Nazi terrorist organization.

In September 1994, Reed wrote in *Prison News Service* that Warden Tate had forced William Rogers, a 17-year-old, 135-pound African-American prisoner convicted on a non-violent crime, into a cell with a "well-known white-supremacist" serving two life sentences for murder. The white supremacist, who "had never been actively violent towards blacks," warned prison officials that if they placed the "nigger" in his cell that he would "kill" him.

According to Reed's article, "As Rogers began to step into the cell, he was immediately struck in the eye with a blunt object by the white man. He ran down the range screaming for the guards to help him, which they did after he was sufficiently assaulted. They took him to the infirmary to have his injuries treated and then escorted him to solitary confinement after charging him [Rogers] with fighting...even though he never even attempted to fight the white man."

Reed insisted in his article, "The Ohio government has targeted me for political imprisonment." Reed remains at large. He has emerged as a well-known spokesperson for Native American prisoner rights and increasingly a cause celeb for international human rights activists.

Update: After being extradited to Ohio in December 1998, Reed was found guilty of four counts of violating his parole. He was sentenced to serve a minimum of six weeks, the remainder of his parole, at the house of his mother.

October 8, 1998

Keeping The Faith

Inspired by President George Bush's praise for "a thousand points of light," Linda Leisure was swept up by the wave of "volunteerism" in the late 1980s and early '90s. Putting aside her fears, the Pentecostal minister worked up the nerve to visit Death Row inmates throughout Ohio she felt needed her spiritual guidance. Similar to Sister Helen Prejean, the real-life nun Susan Sarandon portrayed in the film *Dead Man Walking*, Leisure listened to the condemned men's stories and ministered to their spiritual needs.

Little did Leisure know that the wages of her free spiritual guidance would be the total destruction of her affluent, middle-class lifestyle. The "naive" Leisure who supported the Bush administration's "feel-good" policy initiative has given way to the cynical anti-government "survivalist" Leisure of today. What she saw on Death Row, and what she reported to authorities about Death Row justice, has her now talking about "selling all my earthly belongings and moving to North Dakota."

She's currently representing herself in a lawsuit brought by a former investigator at the Ohio Public Defender's Office (OPDO), whose lawyer admits that they'd be willing to drop their defamation suit if Leisure would just shut up and sign a "confidentiality" agreement or "gag order."

Leisure, standing alone on her conscience, has so far refused to be silenced while also demanding that every judge in the Franklin County Court system recuse themselves because of the peculiar and interlocking relationships that may have compromised their integrity. Leisure's story—supported in well-buried public documents—can only be described as: "The Dirty Little Secret of Ohio's Death Row."

So, as the *Columbus Dispatch* runs positive coverage of Attorney General Betty Montgomery's efforts to "polish up Old Sparky," the nickname for Ohio's long-dormant electric chair, the last remnants of the public concerned with the morality of the death penalty might want to consider the case of *Fox Investigations v. Linda Leisure*. The outcome of the case could determine whether Ohio kills an innocent person.

While volunteering as a Death Row minister, Leisure became involved with helping the wife of Death Row inmate John Spirko prove her husband's innocence. The Spirko case piqued Leisure's interest in investigating murder cases and, in 1994, she decided her talents might be better used in ensuring that justice was being done in individual cases rather than preaching to the condemned. So Leisure took a job with Fox Investigation Inc., a private investigating firm headed by Richard H. Smith, an ex-Columbus police officer and a former investigator at the OPDO. Fox Investigation often did contract work for the OPDO investigating the cases of Death Row inmates.

Leisure did not know the reasons Smith was no longer a cop or state investigator. But she quickly found out why. Soon after going to work at Fox, Leisure claims that Smith "wanted me to falsify time records and interviews on these murder cases." Appalled, she was convinced that certain Death Row inmates were being denied basic "due process" guaranteed them under the Constitution. And, even more frightening, that as a result some innocent American citizen might be executed. This spurred her into action.

Leisure's current woes began with a letter she sent to Common Pleas Judge James J. O'Grady, dated October 25, 1994, in which she alleged that Smith asked her to inflate the investigative bill she submitted to the court. The next month she made these same allegations during a polygraph examination—and passed the exam.

But, as Leisure explains, it was politics as usual in the Franklin County Courts; nobody took her accusations seriously and Smith continued to do business.

Leisure tried desperately to take the story to the press, with no luck. Depressed and nearly defeated, she picked up a copy of the alternative journal *Columbus Free Press*. She claims God spoke to her and told her that the *Free Press* would publish the story because "no one else in Columbus will." The volunteer staff of the *Free Press* agreed to look into Leisure's far-fetched mission from God if she could supply written documentation of her claims.

As if by divine intervention, Leisure learned that she shared the same attorney, Richard Lord, as Chester "Briss" Craig, a former deputy investigator at the OPDO. Craig informed Leisure that he had been Smith's boss at the OPDO and had complained to the Ohio Inspector General with similar concerns—and that there was indeed a paper trail.

Leisure managed to track down a complete copy of the redacted, or blacked out, state investigative report based on

Craig's 1992 complaint to the Ohio Investigator General. With Craig filling in the names, she was able to verify that there existed essentially the same allegations against Smith when he worked at the OPDO.

The report was none too kind to her old boss, either. During his tenure from April 1983 to November 1988 at the OPDO, Smith was allegedly fond of referring to black defendants as "niggers" and white ones as "scumbags," according to the report.

The report shattered Leisure's faith in the Public Defender's Office, but convinced the *Columbus Free Press* to write a story about Craig's experiences at the OPDO. Leisure and the *Free Press* set out to verify Craig's allegations about Smith's sexual misconduct as a Columbus police officer. As Leisure sought the paperwork from the Internal Affairs Bureau of the Columbus Division of Police, prison inmates began to warn her that someone was contacting them, seeking dirt on her.

Following the January 1995 publication of the *Free Press* article, both Leisure and Judy Kendrick, another source for the story, found themselves entangled in lawsuits. Leisure began to receive harassing and threatening phone calls; someone mailed drugs to her house; her attorney Richard Lord said he couldn't represent her anymore; and Fox Investigation and Richard Smith sued Leisure for $150,000 in damages due to his loss of reputation. Leisure found it difficult to hold a steady job due to the harassment and had to re-mortgage her home in order to pay her bills.

"Dick Lord was a good friend, but he told me it was all getting too much for him to deal with, with the drugs and all being mailed to my home. Nobody wanted to help me at that point. But I was determined to expose the immorality of Richard Smith," recalls Leisure.

Leisure was driven as well by the injustice done to Death Row inmates that Craig had told her about and that the highway patrol's investigative report seemed to support. Leisure saw the report not as an obscure testament to the monumental injustices perpetrated by the investigators at the Ohio Public Defender's Office, but as a new challenge. In her mind, the OPDO had betrayed the trust of indigent clients—the men who, is Leisure's eyes, were the "least of my brethren." Now she feared, more than ever, that some possibly innocent person was awaiting execution because of the gross misconduct of investigators and public officials.

Leisure believed that God was directing her to bring the report to public attention. "I talk to anyone who'll listen about my story, hoping and praying that somebody somewhere will do God's will and write about it," Leisure said.

By September 1996, Leisure was laboring alone against Smith and his lawyer, and managed through sheer persistence to force the Columbus police to turn over Smith's 1981 Internal Affairs file that the department had originally claimed "no longer existed." Once again, Leisure was able to verify in detail allegations that Craig had made against Smith.

An investigative summary of Internal Affairs Bureau case number 81-149 regarding "misconduct on the part of Richard Smith" noted: "On October 9, 1981, and during the next five working days, seven (7) female victims were interviewed and they identified Officer Smith as the person who exposed himself to them on October 9, 1981."

In police report number 061278, Missy, a 17-year-old

female, alleges that a suspect she later identified as Smith stated, "Look what I have." The report states: "Suspect was sitting in his vehicle with his pants unzipped and his penis out playing with it."

Donna, 17, was walking her seven-year-old sister and eight-year-old female cousin to Schiller Park in German Village when a suspect in a green car later identified as Smith graphically asked her for oral sex and appeared to be "masturbating in his car," according to the police report.

Thirty-year-old Kathy was pushing her infant daughter in a stroller when a suspect later identified as Smith, according to police report number 061281, "stated 'Nice ass' and began masturbating."

Carol, 23, claims in police report number 061684 that a suspect, later identified as Smith, "had his pants pulled down below his buttocks exposing himself."

According to an Internal Affairs memo, on October 10, 1981, Smith admitted himself to Ohio State University Hospital. These October 9 allegations against Smith, coupled with previous reprimands for various acts of misconduct, including allegedly engaging in sex while on duty, ended his career as a police officer. Within two years, he would be working for the OPDO.

After perusing Smith's Columbus police files, Leisure contacted another attorney, who told her, "Quite frankly, after review of such file, I believe Mr. Smith would have great difficulty proving to a jury that any action by Miss Leisure caused damage to his reputation." As Leisure explains it, standard legal principle asserts that "one must first have a good reputation before it can be damaged."

In 1997, Kendrick settled with Smith and agreed to a gag order. Smith's attorney, Steve Edwards, offered a similar deal to Leisure, she said; they would dismiss their suit against her if she would just shut up and sign a legal agreement never to speak about Smith professional practices again.

Leisure still insists she's moved by the Holy Spirit and driven by her fundamental Christian morality—she says she possesses a "prophetic vision" that allows her to speak "truth to power." Like the Old Testament prophets, she refuses to be silenced with injustice all around her. And like the Old Testament prophet Job, she sees herself being tested.

This year she filed papers to move her case to federal court, although she is not hopeful of the outcome. She's resigned to the fact that she may lose her home if Smith prevails in the Franklin County court system.

"I'm prepared to lose everything except my soul," Leisure lamented. "I think we may be entering that period known as the 'time of sorrows' predicted during the final days, and I'm preparing myself for it."

Dayton Voice
December 17, 1998

The Jailhouse Became
A Death House

When 19-year-old Michael Hiles died in the early morning on September 11, 1998, while incarcerated in a medical isolation cell at the Franklin County Jail downtown, his parents demanded to know why.

More than four months later, Bob and Ruth Hiles refuse to accept the "official" version of their son's death. Aided by Michael's aunt, Cynthia Lee Hiles, the family has raised a multitude of questions concerning the practices of the Franklin County Sheriff's Department and the events surrounding Michael's mysterious death. As far as the family is concerned, the answers to their questions, and the investigation's sometimes contradictory evidence, have yet to be explained.

Franklin County Sheriff Jim Karnes declined to comment for this story. "I can't comment due to pending litigation," he said.

On January 11, Cynthia Hiles, a freelance journalist, sent a massive report titled "Preliminary Investigative Brief on the Deaths and Beatings in the Franklin County Jails, Columbus, Ohio (state capital)" to nine federal agencies, including the U.S. Justice Department and the FBI. She also forwarded a copy to the Franklin County Prosecutor's office. *Columbus Alive* obtained a copy of the brief and a videotape shot by a sheriff's deputy at the county jail death scene in our attempt to investigate Hiles' death.

Michael Hiles is the mixed-race son of Ruth Hiles and his adoptive father, Bob. "I met Michael when he was two. I'm the only father he ever knew and I adopted him when he was nine," his father explained.

As Bob Hiles tells the story on his website, "My son was an alcoholic and a drug addict. His teenage years consisted of inpatient and outpatient therapy at various facilities across central Ohio."

His latest problem began last spring when Michael, "after a binge of intravenous cocaine use," robbed a gas station "with a TV dinner box on his hand" and no gun. His take: $87 and three packs of cigarettes.

Facing up to eight years in prison for robbery, Hiles' attorney arranged a deal whereby Michael would spend two months at the Orient State Correctional Institute and six months at the Maryhaven Adult Drug and Alcohol Rehabilitation Facility. Michael was released on a recognizant bond and resided with his parents in Grove City awaiting incarceration.

On August 11, 1998, Bob Hiles "made the hardest decision of my life. I called our family attorney...and requested to have my 19-year-old son's recognizant bond revoked." In an interview with *Alive*, Bob Hiles stressed that he was practicing "tough love" and had his son's best interests at heart.

On the family's website, he wrote: "My son Michael had been getting up during the night and taking the car after we had fallen asleep. He was out driving drunk and high on drugs in the Columbus area. I feared that Michael was going [to] hurt himself or an innocent bystander."

Bob Hiles, fearing for the safety of his son and others, drove his child to the Franklin County Courthouse on August 14, where he was placed in the custody of the Franklin County Sheriff's Department and incarcerated in the downtown jail. "On September 11, 1998, three days before my son was to appear in court, the Franklin County Jail gave me back my son in a body bag," Bob Hiles wrote. "This was my thank you?"

By all accounts, Michael was positive and upbeat when he headed off to jail. The troubled youth saw his imprisonment as a turning point in his life. In a series of "silly poems" and letters "Mikey" sent home to his wife Cindy and their two young children Allexis and Nicole, his attitude seemed well-adjusted. In a poem titled "New Beginnings," he wrote: "In the next year or so, I'll be known as 'Mike the Goalsetter.'" In another, "Peek-A-Boo," he sent his "three beautiful girls" a picture he drew with a poem that ends: "And one last thing to my baby girls Allexis and Nicki-poo, Peek-a-Boo, I wish I could see you too."

Described by family and friends as "bright," Michael occupied his time by constantly reading while in jail. He wrote his wife the day before his death that "I have read more books in these past three weeks than I've read [in] my whole life. I will come out smarter at least. That I'm sure of. If I keep going at the rate I'm at now, I will have read 80 books by the time I get out. 80!"

Michael Hiles would never meet his projected goal. Two unmailed letters in his cell, both dated September 11, suggest a dramatic shift of mood. A letter to the judge, written earlier that evening, said, "I now have started to find God in my life. It seems like he is my last hope within myself. Hopefully with his help and blessing I will conquer and overcome the 'bad Mike.' Mam [sic], I just ask that the time you give me somewhere...will help me with my problem and not keep my away from the reason I keep myself alive, my family."

The other letter had timelines beginning at "11:45 p.m." and ending at "2:55" a.m.—this last time is just 40 minutes before Franklin County Deputy Timothy Mace claimed he found Michael hanging from the door of his cell by a sheet with both feet on the floor. The letter begins: "Hello honey, I'm in tears right now, again. I can't take this crap anymore, Cindy. Now I am a snitch, that's why I am in here, because I snitched on some drug dealers. That is what these two punks are telling everybody. Now I'm really gonna have problems with people. This guy is telling these lies because he thinks he is cool or something."

Michael was in a medical isolation Cell 10 because of a past history of hepatitis B, not because he had informed on anyone. Tony Alexander occupied Cell 13 and later told the family on tape that inmate Jeffrey Jackson was "taunting" other inmates and claimed to have "some inside information about your son's girlfriend and her kids."

"I don't know what to do. AAAAAAAAHHHHHHH-HH! I hate it," Michael wrote his wife. "These people are all uneducated bastards. I'm down in my cell trying to mind my own business and they are all talking crap about me. Trying to get me worked up.... He said he is going to wreck my home life. That [when he] gets out he is going to rape you. How stupid is that. It is 3-4 guys verse [sic] me."

At "1:30," Michael wrote: "These guys say how there [sic] gonna get your name and address from the envelope when they set it out on the counter. They keep saying they heard me say where you worked and they are gonna send someone up there. God! They won't quit.... They keep calling you a bitch and whore and that all women cheat and that your [sic] out screwing right now. It is not that I believe them but it's just that they keep going and going. They call me a sissy and this and that."

Alexander later told the Hiles family, "Yeah, he [Jackson] was up there talking about he was going to take his girl and he said that his kids wasn't his anyway 'cause they didn't look mixed."

Rickie Cook in Cell 3 West 11, the cell next to Michael, told Lieutenant Larry Winters, the detective who was investigating Hiles' death, that Jackson "was talking about um, fucking his woman and doing this for his kids and doing this to his kids and I'm like, it was wrong."

The last words Michael Hiles wrote were: "I only spoke when he mentioned grandpa. Other than that since the deputy was last around I have shut up. I don't know why he's on there [sic] side. They are all assholes, Cindy. Well I'm gonna go. I'll write you back tonight. I love you baby."

A Franklin County Sheriff's Office routing sheet for correspondence, dated September 11, 1998, recorded that Deputy Mace responded to a Code Blue medical "hanging." Mace's incident report states that he found Michael Hiles at "0335 hours."

Mace reported, "I noticed inmate Michael Hiles #9828170 standing with his back to the door of his cell. Upon closer examination there was a sheet tied to the bars above the door and around his neck. I climbed up on the bars and untied the rope from the bars. I contacted the Control Center to open cell door after inmate Hiles had fallen to the floor and I untied the sheet around his neck. I attempted to awaken inmate Hiles."

The computer cell gate logs do not show this activity. The third floor west area was reset at 2:32:49 a.m. and not activated again until 6:30:06 a.m. Bob Hiles wondered why the computer logs of gate activity could be so inaccurate.

Bob Hiles also finds it interesting that Mace used the terms "sheet" and "rope" interchangeably to describe what was hanging his son. "The marks on his neck didn't look like they were from a sheet. The supposed sheet marks are only around the front of his neck, not the back. Plus, he had bruises all over his body including a deep tissue bruise on his back," Bob Hiles remarked.

Records indicate that Deputy Mace was ordered off the scene at 3:41 a.m. and he never returned.

"EMSA [jail staff] started CPR 03:36," the routing sheet noted. "CFD [Columbus Fire Department] arrived 03:47 and pronounced [Hiles dead] 03:59."

The Columbus EMS report says that Michael Hiles was "found hanging from cell door by sheet at 3:30," six minutes earlier than the deputy's report—crucial minutes when you're going without air.

The Hiles family, despite a less than forthcoming sheriff's department, has managed to piece together an amazing assortment of evidence portraying Michael's final moments.

Bob Hiles wonders why, just after midnight, the computerized logs that record the deputy's rounds show that a deputy spent 81 minutes on the west wing of the third floor between 12:47 a.m. and 1:28 a.m., two hours before Michael's death. The next three listed rounds were all in the two-to-three-minute range, although there was no entry on the third floor west at the time of Michael's death. Bob Hiles told *Columbus Alive* he wants to know whether the computer report was faulty or whether there was a way to manually generate or alter the report.

When sheriff's deputies initially contacted *Alive* to talk off the record about Hiles' death, they repeatedly referred to a videotape which showed, in one deputy's words, "They stood around and let that kid die. It's right on the tape."

The videotape obtained by *Alive* shows Michael laying on his back on the floor halfway out of the door of his cell. Curiously, he's clad in plaid boxer shorts with white underwear underneath and white socks. There's no sign of the orange institutional jumpsuit or of the reported sheet that his parents were told he used to hang himself.

At 3:37:28 a.m., one deputy asks, "Is he breathing?" Another responds, "Not sure" and says that Michael was "hanging from the door, [and] had his feet on the ground."

At 3:38:08, a male nurse, Pearley Gable, arrived. At 3:38:54, a female nurse, Pam Martin, enters the scene. A few seconds later, the male nurse says "Yeah" when asked if Michael has a pulse. A deputy barks, "Call squad."

At 3:40:43, the male nurse clearly states, after examining Hiles with a stethoscope, "He has a pulse. A slight pulse." At 3:40:58—more than three minutes after the first nurse arrived—mouth-to-mouth resuscitation begins. At 3:41:31, the male nurse begins chest compressions as the female nurse watches. At 3:44:38 the male nurse stops CPR and the video camera is clicked off at 3:46 exactly.

The tape begins recording again 32 seconds later as deputies stand around. At 3:47:21, a voice asks, "You want our people to do CPR?"

At 3:47:58 a.m., an order is given: "You can discontinue tape."

The videotape is turned off for nearly three minutes, but video resumes at 3:50:55 as an EMS squad arrives from the Columbus Fire Department. At 3:51:54, an EMS medic asks, "Did you bag him or anything?" in reference to a breathing bag used in the CPR procedure. The answer is "no." At 3:53:09, the EMS medic asks the male nurse, "Want to help...out here bagging or compression ...?"

At 3:59 a.m., Michael Hiles is pronounced dead.

In an interview with Detective Winters, Gable said Hiles' body "was still fairly warm." Martin, who did little to assist Gable even after he said he had a "pulse," wrote a brief report including the sentence: "Other nurse began CPR."

On the original routing sheet under "Follow-Up Remarks," a note reads: "Appears all procedures and policies followed by deputies." According to Franklin County Administrative Regulations, "All personnel at the correctional facility shall receive or have received American Red Cross or equivalent training in emergency first aid and lifesaving techniques within 60 days of employment." In the American Red Cross' publication "CPR for the Professional Rescuer," a subheading titled "When to Stop CPR" states, "Once you begin CPR, try not to interrupt the blood flow you are creating artificially." It also spells out procedures for "Two-Rescuer CPR" and notes that "When two professional rescuers are available, give two-rescuer CPR."

Bob Hiles wants to know why, when his son was found

with a pulse, did the deputies who were presumably trained in CPR stand around and why did only one nurse attempt to resuscitate his son. "Anybody watching that tape is going to see that they didn't care whether he lived or died. They're just standing around and the one nurse is doing little or nothing."

Franklin County Deputy Coroner Dr. Patrick Fardal ruled the death "suicide," writing that the "victim allegedly hanged himself" and the immediate cause of death was "suspension hanging." As he explained during a meeting with the family (which the family recorded on audiotape), "This ruling was 'based on police report.'"

Fardal, according to the Hiles, persuaded the family to have an autopsy and call an attorney to protect their rights. When the family asked the deputy coroner why, he told them, "I'm a realist.... When you're in jail, you're under a different type of care.... Are they following the rules and regulations and doing all the stuff they're supposed to do?"

The grieving father has more disturbing, unanswered questions. He pointed out to *Alive* that on the original incident report, there is no mention of a bedsheet, nor is it listed on the impound form. "It's not on the [video]tape, it's not on the incident report and it's not on the impound form. Suicides are supposed to be treated as crime scenes until the coroner rules otherwise," Bob Hiles said. "Watch that tape. They never treated this as a crime scene. The deputies weren't concerned about evidence. Where's the sheet?"

When the family asked Fardal directly how he felt about the marks around Michael's neck and whether it was consistent with a sheet hanging, the deputy coroner replied,

"It's not as consistent with the sheet as I'd like it to be, per se. But I don't say it's not a sheet." Fardal is clear what evidence he would have preferred to have in making his ruling: "The actual sheet."

According to a report signed by Corporal John Myers, the bedsheet was impounded with personal items from Michael's cell by Sergeant Paul Theodore at the request of Detective Winters. Still, the impound form did not list the sheet. There are two nearly identical impound forms. The first lacks an evidence log number; a second has number 98-1044.

When the Hiles family pressed for the sheet as evidence, a third impound form finally appeared, number 98-1044-A. The form, allegedly dated September 11, 1998, lists a "white sheet" and a different time of death. The first two forms list the official time of death as 3:59 a.m. but the third form lists time of death nine minutes earlier at 3:50 a.m.

Odder still, while the third form is clearly dated "9/11/98," the writing on the form appears upside down and backwards. When the other side of the form is held up to a light, the numbers are right side up, forward and read: "9/18/98." Bob Hiles called this "suspicious," as if the third form was altered or pre-dated.

In Detective Winters' investigative report #9808390, the report the coroner consulted in his finding of suicide, Bob Hiles pointed out several "misrepresentations of facts." Winters wrote that ligature marks appear on the neck, evidence that the medics had been working on the subject."

Deputy Coroner Fardal refers to Winters' ligatures as "nine abrasions that are several inches in length," according to Bob Hiles. Fardal told the family on audiotape that they could have been made by fingernails and that there was superficial bleeding from them. "This means Michael's blood would have to be on the sheet," his father remarked.

Winters also incorrectly wrote, and the videotape shows otherwise, that "When [Columbus] medics arrived, they stated they thought they had a slight pulse; however they could not revive him." This is not factually supported by the tape or the EMS report, although it tends to shift the blame away from the inactive deputies and nurse and toward the EMS medics.

Winters specifically refers to "the actual sheet" and claims in his report it's impounded—two months later, Fardal told the family he would like to see the "actual sheet" to see if it was consistent with the abrasions on Michael's neck.

"The body of Mr. Hiles was rolled to check his back, legs and arms; and we found no signs of any trauma, no bruises or scratching," reads Winters' report.

The autopsy, however, found a deep tissue back injury: "There is an ecchymatic area along the right lateral thorax measuring three-and-a-half by three inches." There were also contusions on Michael's right hand. Bob Hiles ponders whether the imprint on Michael's back was someone's heel, since the deep tissue bruising would most likely be caused by blunt force.

Winters' report also included the following oddity: "He [Michael] had on a set of green and red plaid Tommy Hilfiger shorts, white shorts underneath those, no other clothing." Jail inmates by policy are only allowed to have white underwear.

"Where did this pair of plaid underwear that Michael wore the day he was taken into custody come from?" Bob Hiles asked. "By their own reports, he's not on a suicide watch. Where's his orange jumpsuit? Where's the bedsheets? It's like someone took his clothes off to hide evidence and put him in the plaid underwear he surrendered the first day he came in. It's absurd."

The absurdities, contradictions and apparent procedural irregularities have made the Hiles family more determined to uncover the facts surrounding their son's death. While they concede that certain evidence points to Jackson's taunting possibly inciting Michael's hanging, that's an all-too-convenient answer. Many questions remain unanswered concerning the policies and practices at the Franklin County Jail. But Michael's family pledges to keep on pushing for answers.

Maybe Michael sensed this when he wrote the poem "Love Is," which ends: "So in the end when I pass away and my last breath, you can turn to our kin and say, Love is there still, even in his death."

January 21, 1999

"He Ain't Faking It"

In exploring the as-yet unproven possibility that Michael Hiles died from either a severe beating or lack of medical attention, journalist (and Michael's aunt) Cynthia Lee Hiles presented a massive report to nine federal agencies. As part of that report, Cynthia Hiles put together a list of nine inmates who have died in the Franklin County Jail since May 1994. Four of the inmates were in isolation cells.

Perhaps none of Cynthia Hiles' findings is more alarming than the 1996 case of Gregory Chesney, whose story was leaked by deputies from inside the jail. A report by Lieutenant Robert West on November 23, 1996, noted, "The medical staff at CCH [Columbus Community Hospital] were saying the inmate had been beaten while in jail.... One officer stated he was told by a nurse the inmate had a bruise on his chest that appeared to be a shoe print."

Detective James W. McCall interviewed CCH nurse Mici Petrovic. His report stated, "She informed me that inmate Chesney was suffering from malnutrition, dehydration, a punctured lung and had been beaten up. She then showed me his right leg which had some bruising and his left thigh which had been bruised severely. Inmate had various small and large bruises on lower part of back, left bicep, left ribcage. She also informed that inmate had a swollen groin.

I then asked her if he could have received these injuries from falling down."

Chesney, like Michael Hiles, was found in an isolation cell.

After McCall's damning report, Lieutenant Larry Winters took over the Chesney investigation. After interviewing a severely injured and disoriented Chesney, who provided "a 15-minute rambling statement," Winters concluded that "Mr. Chesney is unable to give any answers to these questions and gave no indication that he did receive these injuries from anything but self-inflicted injuries. At this time I'm going to clear this report unfounded. There is no criminal activity."

Chesney died some months later from his injuries.

In her brief to federal agencies, Cynthia Hiles wrote: "I saw the eight photographs of Gregory Chesney's body and I went through the autopsy of my nephew, Michael Jason Hiles, with Dr. Patrick Fardal, Franklin County [Deputy] Coroner. I am not an expert in this field, but common sense shows an unlearned individual such as myself that these individuals were beaten, yet Detective Larry Winters closed the cases as he did many of the other cases of abuse I read."

In addition to details of the nine dead inmates, Cynthia Hiles supplied data on four alleged gang-style beatings by deputies on inmates and 32 allegations of deputies using excessive force and picking fights with inmates in 1998. There were also five cases last year where deputies reported other deputies for abusive behavior towards inmates.

Cynthia Hiles also forwarded four cases involving the alleged lack of medical treatment for inmates. This includes the shocking case of Ronnie Valentine, who died at Franklin County's Jackson Pike jail after "the subject basically bled to death through his esophagus and intestinal tract," Cynthia Hiles' report states.

Valentine's cellmate, Tony Marcum, told Detective Winters that Valentine had been throwing up "a fountain of nothing but blood...for two days through." Marcum claimed a deputy ignored his plea for help and it was so bad that he gave Valentine trash bags to throw blood up into.

"He didn't want to go to court and the nurse come in, took his blood pressure and says, oh, he's capable, and then a deputy was standing there and said, c'mon, quit faking it," Marcum stated. "I was like man, he ain't faking it, man, I'm telling you he's been throwing up blood all night."

January 21, 1999

Right To Life

Wilford Berry—one of God's most wretched creatures—is scheduled to die on February 19, 1999. If the state of Ohio murders Berry, charges should be brought against Attorney General Betty Montgomery for crimes against humanity.

Berry, diagnosed in the past as delusional with a schizophreniform disorder and chronic undifferentiated schizophrenia, is using the people of Ohio to commit suicide. Shockingly, Montgomery is all too willing to play the obedient German from the Nazi era. Remember, it was the Nazis who rounded up the disturbed and mentally ill and gassed them. Betty, after consulting the pollsters, prefers lethal injection. Pick your poisons, I suppose.

Where are the so-called "right-to-lifers" and the Christian Coalition? Well you can find one, the most Reverend David Chase, on the front page of Saturday's *Columbus Dispatch* Metro section. Chase, in the name of Jesus, is serving as a cheerleader for Berry's suicide. The *Dispatch* duly reports Chase's religious hypocrisy in their steady drumbeat to keep the dead man walking.

The Reverend Chase described his role as "lead[ing] people to Jesus" and "into eternal life." He might have simply called himself Reverend Kevorkian.

The *Dispatch* quotes Chase as saying, "I told him [Berry]

I'd see him in about 80 years up in heaven." Let's see. The holy man is encouraging a mentally ill and brain-damaged convicted killer to waive his constitutional rights and commit suicide. I doubt it'll be in heaven when they finally meet again.

Chase, working with his co-conspirator, the *Dispatch*, cites Paul's letter to the Romans in defense of the death penalty. Chase, the Christian minister, conveniently fails to cite the words of Christ. Why? Because there's no true Christian theological justification for his born-again heresy.

But the real culprit here is the *Dispatch*. As the hour of execution approaches, the daily newspaper repeatedly fails to refer to the basic fact surrounding Berry's crime—the killing of Charles J. Mitroff Jr. on December 1, 1989. An accomplice of Berry's, now serving life in prison, reportedly fired the first and fatal shot. The deranged Berry, under the misguided assumption that Mitroff wanted to kill his sister, agreed to confess to the murder only if he could receive the death penalty.

If you doubt my indictment of the *Dispatch*, let me refer you to Sunday's paper, with the blaring headline: "Mother of slain guard wanted to see Berry die." We are told in a subhead that "Wanda Vallandingham pushed for the execution of 'the Volunteer' before her death." A quick glance at these headlines implies that Berry had something to do with the slain guard at Lucasville. Of course he didn't. Rather, Death Row inmates broke out of their cells and savagely beat Berry because he was "the Volunteer." Berry was a victim of the Lucasville riot as was Vallandingham's son.

Why would any responsible newspaper in America run such scurrilous yellow journalism with an execution pend-

ing? The only story here is that the grief-stricken, emotionally distraught Wanda Vallandingham sought
vengeance and wanted to see somebody—anybody—die
before she did. Why is the *Dispatch* exploiting a deceased
woman in the paper's crusade to whip up public fervor to
kill Berry?

Hate, fear and vengeance are hot buttons that sell news-
papers. Being tough on crime and oral sex is just about all
the Republican Party has left on its agenda. And it helps
that Berry puts a white face on the death penalty. Only 87
of the 191 men on Death Row in Ohio are white—and
every single one of them is indigent.

On Monday, the former evil empire, Russia, announced
that it is doing away with the death penalty. In Ohio, we're
moving in the opposite direction. Of the 200 or so nations
on earth, only a handful would dare kill a brain-damaged
mentally ill man—perhaps Burma and Iran, and of course,
the most uncivilized country of all, the United States.

What's different is that in Burma and Iran they would
try to hide their gross violations of human rights from the
scrutiny of the more civilized nations of world. In the U.S.,
politicians like Betty Montgomery turn it into a public
spectacle and will no doubt set up "I kill the mentally ill"
political action committees to capitalize on Berry's exter-
mination.

Polls show most Ohioans only support the death penalty because there's no true life-in-prison sentence.
Politicians have rigged the sentencing so they can use the
carnival atmosphere of a death sentence to suck you into
their political freak show.

Many lemming-like Ohioans mouth the phrase, "If he
wants to die, we should grant him his wish." I suppose if

prisoners on Death Row just wanted a big-screen TV we should buy them one, too. It would be cheaper for taxpayers than the $3 million to $7 million cost of a typical execution.

Berry needs to be institutionalized for his mental illness and brain damage and not let out until he poses no threat to society. If that means locking him up for life, so be it. In killing the "evil" Berry—who was sexually molested in our state-run institutions as a youth—we become the worst evil, a demented and bloodthirsty society parading around in a clown suit called Christianity, ignoring one of its main tenets: Thou shalt not kill.

February 18, 1999

Stool Pigeons

Attorney Barry A. Mentser filed three lawsuits on May 7, 1999, on behalf of inmates at the Madison Correctional Institution. These lawsuits, filed in the Ohio Court of Claims, and a state investigative report, provide a frightening glimpse into the practices of the Ohio Penal Industries—the state program that administers prison labor—and raise questions about the general direction of Ohio's prison-industrial complex.

Theodore Reddy, Joseph Bowles and Richard Gloden are suing the Ohio Department of Rehabilitation and Correction for negligence. All three inmates worked on an Ohio Penal Industries (OPI) demolition crew at a London Correctional Institution site and, according to court papers, the men all came down with histoplasmosis—a potentially debilitating respiratory disease caused by close contact with pigeon droppings.

Their lawsuits allege that they were required "to work in close proximity to a large amount of pigeon feces and related debris" and they "contracted histoplasmosis at the work-site...and required continuing medical treatment."

The charge of negligence stems from the allegation that the corrections department "did not provide plaintiff[s] with the appropriate training, protective gear, or take any preventative measures to minimize and/or prevent plaintiff[s] from contacting histoplasmosis, pursuant to state and/or federal rules and regulations."

Normally such inmate lawsuits simply provide fodder for right-wing talk show hosts trying to boost ratings. This case should prove different: This time, the inmates' allegations were investigated by a special assistant in the Office of Correctional Health Care, George D. Alexander. Prison working conditions were then detailed in a report from Alexander to Robert O.E. Keyes, the correctional health-care office's deputy director.

Alexander noted in the August 6, 1998, report that he was "informed that in 1997, a work stoppage by outside contractors lasted 47 days due to the threat of contracting histoplasmosis from pigeon droppings and dust." While non-inmate workers wisely refused to be subjected to vast quantities of pigeon feces, the prison industries' virtual slave laborers were required to do the dirty work.

Alexander uncovered three separate inspection reports from a private contractor, Emilcott-dga Inc., warning of the dangers of "pigeon droppings" and recommending specific "precautions." Emilcott issued the first report on November 25, 1997, and the second two weeks later, both during the civilian work stoppage.

As a result of the reports, a training video was made to teach the civilian construction workers how to safely deal with pigeon feces. When Alexander visited the site on August 3, 1998, he learned that a OPI demolition crew had just demolished a restroom at the London facilities; as they removed a wall, "a large quantity of pigeon droppings and dust suddenly fell from behind the wall." An OPI asbestos removal crew was then called in to clean up the area.

Alexander's report describes the interesting scenario when the OPI demolition crew returned: "While I was present, a crew of six OPI demolition workers were sweeping the area and hauling trash to be discarded. I observed that each inmate was wearing a hard-hat. All were wearing tear away paper jumpsuits over their regular clothing, however the sleeves had been removed from the jumpsuits and they were not zipped up. Only one inmate was wearing a dust mask over the mouth and nose and a second had the mask on but it was around his chin. One inmate was wearing safety goggles. One inmate was sitting in a wheelbarrow while taking a break. I was in the area between 10 and 15 minutes. During the entire time no supervisor was present."

In his report, Alexander directly links the lack of supervision and proper safety equipment to prison officials. For a bureaucrat, his comments are remarkably frank: "I viewed the video that is shown each Thursday to new workers. The video appears to be the initial training session that was presented to the construction workers before they returned to work [after the work stoppage]. The presentation is very poor to say the least. The audio is almost inaudible and the video out of focus. A question and answer section is completely inaudible."

Discussions between Alexander and Bob Mouradian, an OPI construction supervisor, revealed that "inmates are not required to 'sign off' when they are instructed in safety procedures and that he [Mouradian] is not aware that training records are maintained on employees," according to the report. Now imagine what would happen to a private sector employee who openly admitted to such violations of state and federal health regulations.

In October 1982, about 1,700 inmates out of a statewide population of 16,400 worked in OPI jobs. Twelve years later, Reginald Wilkinson, director of the corrections department, bragged in a 1994 *Columbus Dispatch* op-ed piece that the "factory-type work supervised by Ohio Penal Industries had increased its prisoners workforce from 2,024 at the beginning of 1991 to 5,079 in the fall of 1994." Wilkinson attributes this to the man who appointed him, then-Governor George Voinovich.

In 1990, there were 20 prisons in Ohio; when Voinovich left the governor's office, there were 31. This year, Wilkinson and Governor Bob Taft proposed a $2.7 billion two-year prison budget. By 2001, Ohio prison spending will be three times what it was when Voinovich moved into the governor's mansion in 1991.

Racial profiling, mandatory sentencing, de-industrializing Ohio and attacks on the working class swelled the prison population. Conveniently, the Voinovich family and their cronies were in the jail- and prison-building business.

But they're not the only ones benefiting from the prison-industrial complex—any industry employing prison workers is getting virtually free labor without occupational safety and health regulations. As Wilkinson wrote, "The new private contracts [for OPI workers] have come in the area of doing work that might ordinarily be sent to workers outside the United States."

Taxpayers are subsidizing an internal banana republic, a primarily black workforce within the Ohio prison system. It's been almost a hundred years since Upton Sinclair wrote his classic *The Jungle*. For the sake of men like Reddy,

Bowles and Gloden, we need a new wave of muck-raking journalists to expose the new horrors of Ohio's prison-industrial complex.

June 17, 1999

Throw Away The Key

This Saturday, May 20, 2000, the fledgling Prisoner Advocacy Network (PAN) will join with the campus-based Copwatch crowd to demonstrate against the prison-industrial complex. The rally couldn't come at a better time. The cover story for the May/June issue of the investigative magazine *Mother Jones* shouts: "Prison, Inc.: How one corporation is turning a rusting steel town into the private-prison capital of the world."

Last year, the top national story recognized by the Association of Alternative Newsweeklies dealt with the same subject—Correction Corporation of America's (CCA) attempt to turn Youngstown into the nation's for-profit prison capital. Who says the Buckeye State isn't world-class?

Tragically, the city that once led the nation in steel production now leads in prison cell "profit unit production." Much like the highly questionable and smelly policy during Governor George Voinovich's regime to allow the importation of garbage and toxic waste into Ohio, CCA "imported 1,700 of the most violent inmates from Washington, D.C." into its Youngstown prisons beginning in 1997, according to *Mother Jones*.

PAN correctly points out in its literature that the prison-industrial complex is race- and class-based, with more than

60 percent of the state prison population so-called minorities, and virtually all coming from lower economic classes. PAN also makes key links between the prison labor industry, which pays 40 cents an hour—Look out low-wage Mexican and Haitian workers, Ohio's coming at you!—and the weakening of labor unions across the country. If the Communist Chinese can masquerade as just another corporate capitalist entity to use prison labor, why can't we?

This may help explain why nearly 12,000 Ohio prisoners are serving sentences well beyond their eligible parole release dates. Five to 10 will get you 10 years in the brave new world of perpetual (and profitable) incarceration.

Back in September 1977, Youngstown Sheet & Tube announced without warning that it would close its Campbell Works, triggering the rapid de-industrialization of the steel town. Now workers can start at CCA's prison for $24,600 a year—much less than the steelworkers made 23 years ago.

The zero-tolerance drug policies launched in the Reagan years, coupled with the "privatization of government services" mantra, led to a tripling of prisoners since the 1970s. *The New York Times* last year noted that many of those now incarcerated are in for low-level drug possession and sales. The rates of drug use in the U.S. and in Western European democracies are virtually identical, while the incarceration rate in Europe for such offenses is almost non-existent.

CCA rushed into the privatization gap, staffing its Youngstown facilities "with guards who had little or no experience in corrections," *Mother Jones* documents. Between 1995 and 1998, 79 inmates escaped from CCA's private prisons, while only nine escaped from the entire California state system, which contains more than twice as many inmates.

Still, you've got to admire CCA's entrepreneurship. It takes a certain amount of business savvy to negotiate a $182 million contract with the District of Columbia to house the area's most violent felons in a state halfway across the country.

Of course, the deal tells us far more about Ohio's elected officials, such as the infamous Representative James Traficant Jr. who, when he's not being investigated by the FBI for alleged organized crime connections, found the time to sign a "memorandum of understanding" in May 1999 to add two more CCA facilities in his district.

Quick, somebody better warn Germany's Deutsche Bank and the Japanese Ministry of International Trade and Industry—Ohio is jumping into re-industrialization in a big, big way!

The United States ranks number two in the world in incarceration rates, according to the think tank The Sentencing Project. For every 100,000 people, the U.S. locks up 600 of its citizens. Compare that to Japan, which locks up 37 of every 100,000 citizens, and Germany, which locks up 85 per 100,000. Even by imprisoning political dissents, the Chinese can only manage 103 incarcerations per 100,000. Only the former Soviet state of Russia tops the U.S. in incarceration rates.

Legendary new left activist Staughton Lynd's Prison Forum recently launched a campaign called "Schools, not jails." There's a novel idea for a state where the Republican-dominated Supreme Court has repeatedly declared the public K-12 educational system unconstitutional because of its blatant disparities and inadequacies.

The many ex-prisoners I've talked with about the rehabilitative power of the prison system, to a man, point out that drug use is rampant inside prison walls. Concentrated, dehumanizing brutalization—with little to no education or job training—is hardly a model for reforming nonviolent, drug-related behavior. But try to explain that to a Prozac nation that worships its drug emporiums. And knows that it's illegal for the lower class to be addicted without a prescription.

I'm getting so nervous and anxious just thinking about the prison-industrial complex, I've got to go now and call that 1-800 number for the drugs they advertise on TV. No doubt some 40-cents-an-hour prisoner in Ohio will take my credit card number as soon as I'm diagnosed over the Internet. God bless free enterprise.

May 18, 2000

Convicted By A Snitch

"The atmosphere of the death house was smothering, suffocating, as if there was a shortage of oxygen. Everybody moved as if in slow motion. Their every move seeming to have been thoroughly rehearsed, learned, robot-like professionalism, as now, for the first time in over 30 years, they, the elite death squad, had been called upon to commit murder in the state of Ohio. In some of these eyes I saw fear, concern, and revulsion—in others, sadistic glee."

These were almost the last thoughts of John Byrd Jr., as he prepared to die in Ohio's electric chair on March 14, 1994. But after narrowly escaping death that night, Byrd lived another day—another six years and counting—and was able to recall in the written statement above what it was like to come face-to-face with his executioners.

Byrd came within 30 minutes of being the first man executed in Ohio since 1963. He lost that historic distinction last year when a well-documented mentally ill and brain-damaged prisoner, Wilford Berry, refused to legally defend himself and entered infamy as the "Volunteer."

Although Byrd was granted a last-minute reprieve by the U.S. Supreme Court, when it upheld his "stay of execution" the evening he was to die, Byrd is likely to be put to death within the next few months. He's run out of appeals.

Columbus Alive's extensive review of court documents indicates that Byrd may die because of the possibly perjured testimony of a jailhouse snitch, condoned by overzealous Hamilton County prosecutors. Arrested with two co-defendants on robbery and murder charges, Byrd was the only one of the three accomplices to receive the death penalty, despite the state's failure to provide any forensic evidence linking Byrd to the murder victim.

Justice is supposed to be meted out evenly and equitably. But as Byrd's case illustrates, justice is too often a game of chance, with steep odds favoring the dealers.

The losers pay with their lives.

On the evening of April 17, 1983, Cincinnati King Kwik convenience store clerk Monte Tewksbury was stabbed once in the side during a robbery. He called his wife and described the robbers as two masked men; he later died in a local emergency room.

In the early morning hours of April 18, 19-year-old John Byrd was arrested along with John Brewer and William Woodall, two ex-felons, in a construction van that contained Tewksbury's possessions.

The evidence seized from the van placed Brewer at the murder scene. Under Brewer's passenger seat was Tewksbury's wife's gasoline credit card. Brewer had in his possession a $20 bill, two $10 bills, four $5 bills, 29 $1 bills and a large quantity of change matching the suspected contents of the King Kwik cash register. Detectives would later find Brewer's shoeprint on the countertop of a store robbed that night.

Sitting in the van next to Brewer was Byrd, with $1.47 in his pocket and no credit cards.

A short time after the King Kwik robbery, two masked men robbed a nearby U-Totem store. A customer, Dennis Nitz, told the police that one of the robbers had a knife and was wearing tan pants and a long-sleeved shirt. Since Byrd was wearing blue pants and a shirt with cut-off sleeves, prosecutors would later argue that the witness was mistaken about the pants' color and that Byrd had cut off his sleeves to hide the blood evidence they couldn't find on him.

The arresting officer noted that while there was no blood on Byrd, there appeared to be fresh blood on the driver's seat where Woodall sat. The Bowie knife purportedly used to stab Tewksbury never materialized; however, a work knife with no blood evidence on it was found in the van.

Byrd has steadfastly maintained that he didn't kill Tewksbury. He's claimed all along that when he woke up in the Cincinnati Correctional Institute the next day, he thought he was there for alcohol-related charges after a night of drinking, smoking pot and doing Quaaludes, according to Richard J. Vickers, his post-conviction attorney supplied by the Ohio Public Defender's office. Even after repeated questioning, neither Byrd nor his co-defendants made any statements to the police admitting the slaying of the store clerk.

Police and prosecutors knew it would be difficult to convict Byrd on a capital murder indictment without any direct evidence linking him to the killing. Not all murderers are equal under the law. Only the most heinous—cold-blooded, pre-meditated—receive capital indictments, with the possibility of receiving a death sentence. But amidst mounting public pressure and sympathetic media portrayals of the victim, who left a widow and three children, it was almost certain that one of the three accomplices would have to die.

Brewer and Woodall, each tried separately, never received a capital murder indictment. Both were eventually convicted by a jury of aggravated murder, but escaped the death chamber and remain in prison.

Events that transpired in the jailhouse and at Byrd's grand jury indictment would transform Byrd into the prosecution's version of the remorseless killer, despite the lack of an eyewitness tying him to the murder, fingerprints or other forensic evidence at the scene, or blood on an alleged murder weapon.

The grand jury that convened to issue indictments in the Tewksbury slaying initially heard testimony that Byrd was the killer from a highly suspect source, according to Vickers. Brewer's sister claimed that her brother told her that Byrd did it.

The state later turned to an even more suspect source in order to convict Byrd at trial on capital murder charges— well-known jailhouse informant Ronald Armstead.

Armstead wrote the prosecutors claiming that Brewer, Woodall and Byrd were openly bragging about killing Tewksbury. He claimed that approximately three weeks after the robbery, Byrd supposedly confessed the cold-blooded nature of the murder to Armstead while the two of them watched a *PM Magazine* segment featuring footage of the singing Tewksbury family.

Conveniently, the confession during the show allowed prosecutors to later show the emotionally wrenching footage of the happily singing family at trial.

It's Armstead's key testimony—portraying Byrd as a calculated, cold-blooded killer—that allowed prosecutors to win a death-penalty conviction. In dramatic testimony, a weeping Armstead told the jury that Byrd confided in him that he killed Tewksbury. "Fuck him [Tewksbury], he deserved to die," Armstead swore Byrd said.

The *Cincinnati Enquirer* reported at the time that Armstead's testimony was the most dramatic of Byrd's trial. The paper wrote, "Observers in the packed courtroom appeared captivated by Armstead and a stunned silence fell over the courtroom."

Daniel "Woody" Breyer, a Hamilton County prosecutor who, with Carl Vollman, tried the Byrd case, concurred. "I've seen it all and I've never seen a courthouse so intent, so rapt, so quiet, so involved," Breyer told *Columbus Alive*. "Tears were coming down [Armstead's] cheeks. He pointed at Byrd, and you could hear a pin drop."

But to believe Armstead's testimony, one has to accept that three white guys suspected of murder, and described by defense attorney Richard J. Vickers as "rednecks," refused to talk to the police but suddenly confessed to Armstead and his fellow black inmates Virgil Jordan and Marvin Randolph in jail. Ronald Armstead, who wept during his testimony, claimed John Byrd confessed to him because he "knew a lot about the law" and that "the white boys bared their souls" to him.

Vickers doesn't buy the story that the white guys confided to three black guys in jail, two of them known snitches. He sees that as an absurd scenario.

"It's 1983 in Hamilton County. My client's a redneck in jail. Is he going to seek out three black cons and confess a murder to them that he steadfastly denied to everybody else?" Vickers said. "As Virgil Jordan, the self-described 'King of the Snitches' put it, you shouldn't put frogs with snakes. They were schooled. They knew just enough facts to make themselves snitches."

As Vickers explained it to *Columbus Alive*, the Hamilton County prosecutors did not have a capital murder case against Byrd until Armstead stepped forward: "Armstead's confession is the only direct evidence they had linking Byrd to the murder. It's the only part the jury asked to re-hear in their deliberations. Forty-five minutes later, they found Byrd guilty on all charges including specifications for the death penalty."

According to Vickers, Armstead had also offered virtual-ly the same dramatic testimony at supposed accomplice John Brewer's earlier trial. In that case, Brewer was the killer instead of Byrd.

Byrd's final appeal to the United States Court of Appeals for the Sixth Circuit was handed down on April 6, 2000. Both the two-judge majority and the blistering dissent focused on Armstead's testimony.

The majority opinion reads: "The main evidence intro-duced at trial to prove that Petitioner [Byrd] was the prin-cipal offender, i.e., the individual who actually stabbed and murdered Monte [Tewksbury], came from Ronald Armstead." The court also conceded, "All agree that Armstead's testimony was vitally important to the jury's determination."

After a 10-day trial that ended on August 12, 1983, the jury had one request for the court: could they have the Armstead testimony read back to them. Over an objection from Byrd's attorney, the court reporter read the entirety of Armstead's dramatic and flamboyant testimony to the jury in open court. Part of what the jury heard was, "And he said, 'Yeah, I killed him, I killed him, you know, because he was in my motherfucking way, fuck him.' You know, that's the whole attitude they took the whole time they were there, they don't care, you know. He [Byrd] don't care. [Pointing at Byrd.]"

The jury was never informed of the state's star witness' dubious past. While Byrd's trial attorneys managed to get into the record that Armstead had been convicted of a felony within the last 10 years, the jury was not aware that Armstead was in jail on a parole violation and was facing a return to state prison for a three- to 15-year stay, nor that his rap sheet of assault convictions was pages long.

Hamilton County prosecutors failed to disclose Armstead's parole violation and pending return to prison as well as his extensive criminal past. Nor did prosecutors disclose Armstead's prison intake screening from 1981, which showed he "possesses below average intelligence and has achieved academically around the third grade."

The Supreme Court has ruled that prosecutors must turn over exculpatory evidence or evidence that could have been used to impeach the state's star witness. But the prosecution had in its possession a three-page parole report that it never turned over in which Armstead admitted to the prison psychologist that "he has been addicted to heroin and Talwin for some 10 years."

By withholding this information from the defendant, the prosecutors prohibited Byrd's attorneys from casting doubt on Armstead's vital testimony. Even worse, when asked if "any charges" were pending against him, Armstead testified, "I don't have no time pending or nothing else pending.... I don't have no more cases pending and I come to testify against [Byrd] because he was wrong."

In the April 2000 Sixth Circuit Court ruling, one judge vigorously dissented against the two-judge majority, arguing that Byrd should have a new hearing. Judge Nathaniel R. Jones wrote in his dissent, "At best, these [Armstead's] statements were misleading and left the jury with a material mis-impression of fact. At worst, these statements were patently false, which the prosecution knew, or should have known." Jones pointedly noted that "'Any' [charges] means 'any.'"

Since John Byrd's original trial, other records withheld from his attorneys have surfaced. These documents demonstrate that the Hamilton County Prosecutor's office was adamantly opposed to Ronald Armstead's parole, and sought to have him returned to prison prior to his testimony against Byrd.

An April 29, 1981, letter from Simon L. Leis Jr., Hamilton County prosecuting attorney to the Ohio Parole Board, stated, "Please be advised that this office strongly opposes any type of furlough, parole or release of defendant Ronald Armstead, aka Ronald Scott, who was committed to your institution a little less than five months ago under a sentence of not less than three years no more 15 years for the crime of felonious assault and trafficking in drugs." Leis pointed out that while incarcerated, Armstead had attempted to escape and attacked both a guard and a nurse "with a metal bed crank."

Leis continued, "We have in the person of the defendant a person who has gone out and committed two prior escapes for which he was convicted and the third time he was convicted of felonious assault and the escape charge was dropped." Leis wrote the Adult Parole Board again in 1982 reiterating the county's position that Armstead should not be paroled.

Vickers suggests that, instead of attacking prison personnel with metal bed cranks, Armstead found an easier way out of prison—as a star witness for the prosecutor's office.

After Armstead's testimony, the Hamilton County prosecutors had a sudden and decisive change of heart and no longer opposed his parole. Daniel Breyer, one of the prosecutors who tried the Byrd case, wrote a letter to the parole board recommending Armstead's release, citing his cooperation in Byrd's conviction.

Breyer told *Alive* that his letter was motivated simply out of concern for Armstead's safety. Armstead contacted the prosecutor and said he was being roughed up in prison because he was a known snitch. "I was worried about Armstead being attacked," Breyer said in an interview this week.

Breyer emphatically denies that Armstead's testimony in the Byrd case was in exchange for early release from prison. "There was no deal," Breyer said. "They'll never prove it. It never happened... It's a fabrication to save Byrd."

"Armstead was returned to prison [after his testimony]," Breyer continued. "If there was a deal, Armstead wouldn't have been returned to prison and I wouldn't have had to write the letter."

Appeals court Judge Jones' dissent argues that Byrd should be allowed to investigate why Armstead, with his pending return to prison, was chosen to testify instead of two other inmates who contacted the prosecutor's office.

The other two inmates have subsequently recanted their stories and denied that Byrd ever confessed to them. They admitted to concocting the story with Armstead in hopes of getting special treatment in jail.

Vickers said that Armstead's friends, Virgil Jordan and Marvin Randolph, both independently supplied affidavits stating that the whole story about the confession was fabricated.

"They felt by snitching it would help them get released from jail. In Armstead's case, it worked, since the parole board reversed itself and refused to send him back to prison, which they initially had planned. Both Randolph and Jordan separately claimed that they knew how to play the snitch game—to write the prosecutor and say that they had 'personal knowledge' of a crime," Vickers explained.

Byrd is in a classic Catch-22, according to Vickers, with the prosecution vouching for the snitch Armstead while telling the court not to believe the two other inmates who originally backed Armstead but now have signed affidavits saying the witness perjured himself. The prosecutor's felon is always the honest felon, according to Vickers.

The majority in the Sixth Circuit Court of Appeals concurred. The two judges pointed out that there are actually statements and affidavits as of April from four inmates alleging that Armstead lied, but they are to be disregarded. "Elwood Jones, Marvin Randolph, Robert Jones and Thomas Sargent are all convicted felons, whose credibility is thereby diminished," the court wrote. The court dismissed their affidavits as "merely impeaching in nature"— of use only to call into question the testimony of Armstead, the state's star witness and also a felon.

"There's a body of case law that says if we can't prove the prosecutor knew or should have known that Armstead perjured himself, then we have no right to a hearing or to depose the prosecutor on the matter," Vickers explained. "This is skewed logic. What prosecutor is going to sign an affidavit swearing that they suborned perjury so we can depose them and discover their documents? It's never going to happen. We'll never have a chance to prove our claims. There's enough in the records to suggest that Armstead was a lying prevaricator simply trying to save his own skin."

Vickers argues that one of Byrd's prosecutors, Daniel Breyer, was in the enviable position of having his brother, William Breyer, as the chief appellate counsel in Hamilton County.

"The court findings that all the subsequent appeals courts have relied on were written and signed by Bill Breyer, who had a stake in protecting his office and his brother's reputation," Vickers offered. "It's the same finding that's been relied on by every appeals court to deny Byrd judicial relief, to deny him a hearing, to deny him the prosecutor's files, to deny him the ability to impeach the testimony of a known criminal and snitch."

So dependent were the prosecutors upon Armstead's evidence linking Byrd to the murder that they "vouched" for his credibility, Vickers contends.

According to court records, during closing arguments one of the prosecutors stated, "[Armstead] looked Byrd right in the face. He looked me in the face. He looked you in the face, Armstead did, he looked the defense attorney in the face and he said, 'What the man did was wrong. He killed that man for no reason.' I'm not sure there's honor among thieves, but I believe Armstead when he took that stand, and I believe you did, too."

The prosecutor's closing argument continued, "Armstead said that he was told by Byrd that Byrd stabbed Monte Tewksbury. I haven't heard any evidence to contradict that. I have seen a lot of circumstantial evidence to support that. I've heard no evidence, direct or circumstantial, to contradict what Armstead said. I believe him, and I submit that you should believe him."

Vickers insisted, "Any time you have the representative of the state telling the jury a witness is telling the truth, it makes for dramatic testimony. It's not evidence, it's the prosecutor's personal opinion. But he's giving the sanction of the state of Ohio to his opinion."

Late last year, Chief Justice of the Ohio Supreme Court Thomas J. Moyer publicly scolded Hamilton County prosecutors in another death-penalty case. "Time and time again we see counsel misconduct which...would appear to be grounds for reversal and the vacating of convictions and/or sentences," Moyer asserted.

"Hamilton County isn't overzealous, it's serious about the death penalty," countered Daniel Breyer, who's now the Clermont County Prosecutor. "We didn't charge people and use it as a bargaining tool [by reducing charges]. We followed through on our obligation and didn't take the easy way out."

In his dissent in the Byrd case, Judge Jones contends, "There's no other way to describe the prosecutor's statement in this case than to use the words 'egregious,' 'astonishing' and 'inexcusable.'" The appeals court judge concluded, "The prosecutory vouching in this case represents flagrant constitutional error."

The majority disagreed, claiming that the federal court "lacks supervisory power over state courts and could only consider 'the fairness of the trial not the culpability of the prosecutor.'" The judges found that there was no legal relief for the prosecutor's "improper vouching" for the state's star witness who they knew was misleading the jury.

Jones' dissent holds that Byrd should be entitled to at least some "limited discovery" in order to find out the facts about the prosecutor's office's relationship with Armstead. "Anything less is a gross and irrevocable miscarriage of justice, as the stark and chilly choice here is between due process or death."

"They're going to kill this guy on this evidence. This raises legal, moral, philosophical and ethical concerns. They're going to kill him although he never received a fair trial," Vickers reflected. "Byrd is going to be executed on that basis. There's no fingerprints, no video, no DNA, no eyewitness linking him to the murder—just his supposed confession supplied by a jailhouse informant."

Meanwhile, Byrd's supposed partners in crime, John Brewer and William Woodall, are sitting safely in prison without any danger of coming near the death chamber. If nothing else, the use of death penalty against only one of the three accomplices is arbitrary at best.

Breyer, needless to say, disagrees. "Just because Brewer, who may have deserved the death penalty, didn't get it, it's no argument that Byrd shouldn't receive the death penalty," the prosecutor said. "Should we do away with putting people in prison because sometimes innocent people are sentenced? The same thing's true of the death penalty."

"No one can argue that Byrd's innocent. It's simply a question of whether the death penalty's applicable or not,"

Breyer continued. "There's no question he did it."

Vickers has been working on the case for 12 years and can't believe it's gone this far towards execution.

Sure, the defense attorney admits, Byrd previously had trouble with the law. He'd run away, stolen a truck, taken it to Kentucky and gone to prison for joy-riding. But the 19-year-old had never committed a violent crime. His mother gave birth to him at 16 and divorced his father soon after because of a jail stint. Her two subsequent marriages failed. One ex-husband was fond of blackening Johnny's eyes, his mother testified. A learning disability made Byrd a subject of frequent ridicule at school, but at the age of 11 he was briefly a local hero when he saved a young child from falling into a frozen creek.

"When the nightmare first began, I was a young, strong, good-looking kid," Byrd wrote from the Mansfield Correctional Institution's Death Row, in a letter received by *Columbus Alive* this week. "The years that have been wasted, spent by enduring...the 23-hour-a-day lockdowns, the mental and physical abuses placed upon me by both the failure of the justice system and the prison administration. The toll of these years upon my physical well-being is expressionless. The parasites that are sucking the life out of my body and plotting my murder can and never will be able to break me! All I want is to be heard and for the truth to be exposed."

"I did not kill this man," Byrd continued. "Taking of life shouldn't rest on the testimony of jailhouse snitches who will and do say anything to gain favor from the prosecutor's office."

John Byrd's impending execution—and a conviction based on the uncorroborated testimony of a single jailhouse informant, felon and possible perjurer—points toward a capricious and farcical system of administering justice. A system where the difference between life and death is just a snitch away.

August 3, 2000

The Sausage Factory

The hot-button capital-punishment debate has become even more contentious in the last year. The rise in use of DNA evidence is garnering the most headlines—freeing wrongly convicted people from Death Rows nationwide—led by a high-profile execution moratorium in Illinois.

How are innocent people landing on Death Row? A June 2000 study by Columbia University law professor James Liebman provides a peek at the answer. In the 28 states Liebman studied, 68 percent of death-penalty convictions were reversed at the federal level because of errors in the judicial process.

Polls indicate that people are increasingly questioning the fairness of the death-penalty process. A June 2000 Gallup poll showed that 66 percent of Americans support the death penalty, down from 80 percent just six years ago. That support may continue to decline drastically, under further scrutiny of state executions. Much like a trip to the sausage factory, Americans may lose their appetite for lethal injection when they learn what really goes on in courtrooms and on Death Row.

A jury sentenced John Byrd Jr. to death without knowing that Ronald Armstead, the trial's key witness, avoided a return to prison after his testimony against Byrd. The jury was misled about the witness' long, violent criminal history, and left with the impression that Armstead's testimony was an unselfish act of civic virtue.

Attempts to cross-examine Armstead about his criminal past were thwarted by prosecutors' objections sustained by the trial court. Thus, jurors could not consider pertinent facts, such as that Armstead had recently committed a crime, had violated his parole, and was facing an impending return to the penitentiary.

He was hardly a selfless citizen doing a good deed.

Such suspect prosecutory behavior caused U.S. Supreme Court Justice Harry A. Blackmun, then the oldest and longest-serving member of the Supreme Court, to announce in February 1994 that he would vote to oppose all future death sentences. He claimed that the system for imposing capital punishment was simply too arbitrary and biased against poor and black defendants to pass Constitutional muster.

"From this day forward, I no longer shall tinker with the machinery of death," Blackmun proclaimed, "I believe that the death penalty, as currently administered, is unconstitutional."

Blackmun's words are those of a judge appointed by President Richard Nixon because of his dedication to "law and order." Blackmun played a key role in restoring capital punishment in 1976, yet he concluded that "the problem is that the inevitability of factual, legal and moral error gives us a system that we know must wrongly kill some defendants, a system that fails to deliver the fair, consistent and reliable sentences of death required by the Constitution."

Three weeks after Justice Blackmun's condemnation of the death penalty, Ohio officials worked feverishly to carry out Byrd's execution, despite his remaining appeals. Then-Attorney General Lee Fisher filed an emergency appeal to the U.S. Supreme Court on March 14, 1994, after conferring with then-Governor George Voinovich, asking the court to allow Ohio's first execution in 31 years.

Byrd waited in his death house cell 13 steps from "Old Thunderbolt," as the *Cleveland Plain Dealer* called it, or "Old Sparky," as the competing *Columbus Dispatch* referred to the electric chair. None of the mainstream news coverage at the time raised the Armstead issues exposed by *Columbus Alive* last week.

Byrd condemned "the apparent unprecedented and mean-spirited tactics being employed by the 'Honorable' Carl Rubin, the judge assigned to my case. It seems that although he had my writ of habeas corpus and motion for a stay of execution before him since March 7, he decided to wait until the '11th hour' before making a ruling, knowing full well that the situation was critical and time was of the essence." The Sixth Circuit Court removed Judge Rubin from handling Byrd's case.

In 1994, after Ohio failed to kill Byrd, then-State Senator Betty Montgomery chaired a panel seeking ways to speed up appeals in death penalty cases. A news account in the *Plain Dealer* documents her utter contempt for an academic witness suggesting that the system was fundamentally flawed. Montgomery invited the family of slain convenience store clerk Monte Tewksbury to testify, and ended up endorsing a constitutional change that outlawed a death penalty appeal to the state appeals court.

Why was the state of Ohio in such a hurry to kill Byrd? Maybe so nosy reporters couldn't dig up Armstead's dubious past and shed light on the suspicious behavior of the

Hamilton County prosecutors. Late last year, Ohio Supreme Court Chief Justice Thomas J. Moyer specifically singled out the Hamilton County Prosecutor's office for its overzealous conduct in pursuing death-penalty cases.

In February, Illinois Governor George Ryan halted executions in his state for a year pending a full investigation of the capital punishment system, one which has admittedly put 13 innocent people on Death Row. Remember, it wasn't the mainstream media that brought the wrongful convictions to light, but a college professor and his students doing research on death penalty cases.

The New Hampshire legislature voted in May to repeal the state's seldom-used death penalty, although Governor Jeanne Shaheen quickly vetoed the proposal. The next month found both the states of Maryland and Virginia commuting or postponing a death sentence because of questions of basic trial fairness.

This, of course, did not stop Texas governor and presidential candidate George W. Bush from carrying out the execution of Gary Graham on June 22, even after three jurors filed affidavits expressing doubts about the lone eyewitness' identification of Graham. Bush's actions drew the condemnation of the ultra-conservative Reverend Pat Robertson.

At the July meeting of the American Bar Association, the group's President-elect Martha Barnett, citing "gross injustice" in the application of the death penalty, called upon the nation's lawyers to support a moratorium on capital punishment. As the lawyers met, President Bill Clinton put the execution of any federal prisoners on hold while the U.S. Justice Department reviews new clemency rules for Death Row inmates and completes a federal death-penalty study.

Concern over the death penalty spread to the Ohio Statehouse as Representative Shirley A. Smith introduced legislation calling for a moratorium on capital punishment in Ohio. Governor Bob Taft immediately dismissed Smith's bill and issued a statement that he has no plans to suspend death-penalty sentences. The governor's spokesperson, former *Plain Dealer* writer Mary Ann Sharkey, informed the media that "He [Taft] believes we have sufficient safeguards with the appeals process and the parole board, and the governor reviews each case."

At the same time that Taft was preaching the superiority of Ohio's capital punishment system, Florida's *St. Petersburg Times* released a study indicating that "the state's registry of death-penalty defense lawyers appears to have been designed to keep Death Row inmates from getting the full defense they are entitled to." Florida Governor Jed Bush supports the system where Death Row attorneys cap their hours at 840, despite a study saying on average they need 3,300 hours to thoroughly defend their clients.

Former Florida Supreme Court Justice Gerald Kogan said, "If you make a mistake in a non-capital case and the defendant is innocent, you can open the prison door. But if you make a mistake in a capital case, you can't dig up" the defendant.

Lacking the Ohio's governor's confidence, a judge in Georgia ordered the body of a man executed four years ago to be dug up for DNA testing a little over a week after Taft's pronouncements. A Virginia judge turned down a similar request earlier in the year.

August 10, 2000

Mental Capacity

At least one positive thing has come from the closely contested presidential recount in Florida: The U.S. Supreme Court stayed the execution of Texas killer Johnny Paul Penry just hours before his state-sanctioned murder was to take place.

Penry is the poster person for the mentally retarded on Death Row. Educated at a home for the mentally retarded, his IQ test scores range between 50 and 63. His attorneys point out that this is the functional level of a six-year-old, that he still believes in Santa Claus, and that he was severely abused as a child.

In 1979, Penry raped and murdered a 22-year-old woman. Initially, a Texas court refused to let the jury even consider evidence of Penry's well-documented retardation in deciding his fate.

Not only have the usual death penalty opponents pleaded to stay the execution, so have the European Union, the American Bar Association and both the American Association on Mental Retardation and the Association for Retarded Citizens. Only a handful of "rogue" nations in the world openly execute the mentally retarded—putting the state of Texas in a league with Mauritius, Tonga and Tunisia. Ohio's Attorney General Betty Montgomery has carved out her own little niche with the execution of

Wilford Berry last year, the "Volunteer" with a long history of mental illness and brain damage from his beating during the Lucasville riot.

Locally, Ohio State University Law Professor Douglas Berman prepared a letter for the Texas Board of Pardons and Paroles claiming, among other things, that "society's 'evolving standards of decency' precludes his [Penry's] execution."

"A 'dynamic' interpretation of the Eighth Amendment to the U.S. Constitution and Article 1, Section 13 of the Texas Constitution, focusing upon 'objective' factors evidencing an evolution of contemporary values over the last decade, leads to the conclusion that the execution of the mentally retarded is no longer tolerated by society's current 'standard of decency,'" wrote Berman.

In the last decade, 13 state legislatures and the U.S. Congress have passed statutes against executing the mentally retarded. In the vast majority of U.S. jurisdictions, Penry would not be killed, according to Berman. Just within the last year, six additional states are considering bills to prohibit the execution of the mentally retarded.

While substantial majorities have continued to support capital punishment, even greater numbers are opposed to the death penalty for retarded people. Berman's letter points to a recent public opinion poll showing that 80 percent opposed the execution of the mentally retarded. Over a decade ago, before it became a hot-button issue, 73 percent of Texans polled opposed the execution of retarded inmates, according to the *Austin American-Statesman*.

Berman suggests that the U.S. Supreme Court likely stayed the Penry execution to allow Texas Governor George W. Bush more time to reflect on the matter. A Texas newspaper reported last week that the governor is busy "playing gentleman rancher at his Crawford spread" and "'enjoying the tranquility of Central Texas,' according to a PR flak."

The *American-Statesman* noted that Bush was "under...unprecedented pressure" from the presidential election recount.

Texas papers seem more than willing to forgive the preoccupied governor for overlooking the obvious moral dilemma posed by executing Penry. Thankfully the Supreme Court proved a little more thoughtful. Arguably, in the U.S., "pregnant chads" should take clear precedence over killing certified retarded people.

The executive director of the Texas Civil Liberties Union said that his state would "shame" itself by killing Penry. The "shame" of killing Penry neither stopped the governor from meeting with architects and builders working on his ranch home nor from grilling hamburgers and reading the new biography of baseball great Joe DiMaggio, according to Bush spokesperson Ray Sullivan.

Ironically, in 1991, Governor Bush's father's President's Committee on Mental Retardation issued a report which concluded that the death penalty was inappropriate for the mentally retarded. Then-President George H.W. Bush authorized the report advocating that "capital punishment be prohibited for persons with mental retardation." Berman cites the report in his letter to the board of pardons.

Perhaps Berman's most telling argument is that last August on *Good Morning, America*, Governor Bush had the following exchange with Jack Ford.

Ford: "Do you personally feel that it's morally repugnant to execute someone who is mentally retarded, regardless of what the legislature would do?"

Governor Bush: "I do—I do feel that way. Yes, I do feel that way."

State's rights aside, it's a good thing the U.S. Supreme Court justices were paying enough attention to justice at hand to save our possible future president from taking office as the killer of a man with the mental capacity of a six-year-old.

November 23, 2000

True Confession

John Byrd Jr. is fighting for his life. Sent to Ohio's Death Row for a 1983 murder he says he didn't commit, Byrd is next in line to sit in the state's electric chair. Now, Byrd's last, best hope for escaping the ultimate irrevocable punishment is an affidavit from another man who says he is the real killer.

Last August, six federal judges on the Sixth Circuit U.S. Court of Appeals dissented from the majority and supported a petition for rehearing Byrd's case.

The facts laid out starkly and precisely by Judge Nathaniel R. Jones in the dissent underscore the grave injustice of the pending execution of John Byrd: "No eyewitness or other physical evidence identifies the particular robbers responsible for the murder, and the only evidence distinguishing the assailants are the representations of a jailhouse 'snitch.' After a trial featuring the snitch's testimony in which the jury inaccurately believed the snitch did not have any jail time or other criminal punishment pending, the person identified by the snitch is found guilty and sentenced to death. The other two perpetrators receive life sentences."

Ronald Armstead, the "snitch," was freed from prison soon after his ludicrous testimony helped send Byrd to Death Row.

Last week's release of a nearly 13-year-old affidavit, in which one of the men serving a life term actually confessed to the killing, should come as no surprise to *Columbus Alive* readers.

Public Defender David A. Bodiker told *Alive* that Armstead, who now floats between San Diego and Las Vegas working as a cook among other things, had previously told authorities another inmate, Billy Joe Sowell, allegedly confessed to him about a killing as well. The fortuitous Armstead was facing up to 15 years in prison for a parole violation after assaulting a nurse and prison guard with a hospital bed crank, when murderers seemed to select him at random to confess for Death Row crimes.

Armstead's testimony, the only direct evidence against Byrd, allowed Armstead to conveniently escape re-incarceration.

During Byrd's trial, Armstead, the former junkie, sex offender and robber, was portrayed as a model citizen whose only motive was to tell the truth in the slaying of Monte Tewksbury, a Cincinnati convenience store clerk. Unbelievably, Armstead, who is black, somehow managed to win the confidence of Byrd, a white 19-year-old, in the highly racially polarized atmosphere of the Hamilton County Jail.

Judge Jones saw it a little differently: "The government led the jury to believe that jailhouse snitch Ronald Armstead faced an eminent release from prison, and therefore had no reason to fabricate testimony against Byrd. Indeed, pursuant to government questioning, Armstead repeatedly told the jury that he had 'no time pending.'" Armstead lied—and the prosecutor vouched for him.

"Nevertheless, after his [Armstead's] testimony, the prosecutor's office informed the state parole board that it did not object to an early release and shortly thereafter, Armstead went home. The government knew the truth, and so did Armstead. The jury did not," Jones succinctly explained.

The appeals court's dissent also points out, "Without any evidentiary predicate, the prosecutor theorized on topics as diverse as the location of the murder weapon, the where-abouts of other unrecovered key evidence."

The prosecutor did this, in part, because the circumstan-tial evidence pointed to John Brewer, who has now sworn twice that he killed Tewksbury. Minus the snitch, Byrd would have been sentenced to life in prison for being pres-ent at the murder scene, rather than death for committing the murder. Byrd has steadfastly claimed that he was drunk and on downers in the robbery van at the time of the crime and never killed anybody.

Bodiker maintains that the nature of death penalty cases and the post-conviction process left no appropriate legal place for Brewer's confession to be admitted. If a majority of the Sixth Circuit bench had supported a rehearing, new evidence may well have come forward. Bodiker describes Byrd's original trial attorney's behavior as "atrocious." The public defender rightly notes that there was a "tremendous amount of prosecutory misconduct" at the original trial, a fact not lost on the six dissenting judges.

"This case also raises whether a capital defendant has received constitutionally effective representation when his counsel fails to challenge prejudicial prosecutory miscon-duct," the dissent reads.

"In the face of...wrongful vouching for Armstead's cred-ibility, and speculation as to facts not in evidence, there cannot be a reasonable norm of capital defense practice that suggests it is strategically appropriate to remain mute in the face of such an assault on the defendant's right to a fair trial," the dissenters correctly conclude.

Perhaps one of the reasons the Brewer affidavit appeared so late in the Byrd proceeding is the outrageous, but often overlooked, incompetence and internal mismanagement in the public defender's office in the mid-1990s, as the *Columbus Free Press* has reported.

The bizarre nature of the scandal can be found in the report by Highway Patrol Trooper Mark Rogols. Former Ohio Public Defender Death Row Investigative Supervisor Chester "Briss" Craig listed the names of 15 Death Row inmates who had been denied due process as a result of botched and forged investigations by investigators for the public defender's office. Byrd's name was prominent on that list. The Rogols report substantially documents this dirty little secret of Ohio's Death Row.

Attorney General Betty Montgomery attacked the re-organized and more effective public defender's office for releasing the Brewer affidavit. If she is truly concerned with justice, she would have welcomed the evidence and demanded a new trial for Byrd. Siding with snitches, encouraging cover-ups and railroading people into the death chamber cannot be tolerated.

February 1, 2001

Fasting Behind Bars

At least 25 prisoners began a hunger strike on March 15, 2001, at the Ohio State Penitentiary (OSP) in an on-going struggle to improve conditions at the state's "supermax" prison. In January, both the American Civil Liberties Union of Ohio and the Center for Constitutional Rights in New York filed a class-action lawsuit in U.S. District Court in Cleveland contending the OSP is unconstitutional.

The suit claims that inmates are locked down for 23 hours a day in spartan seven-foot-by-14-foot cells. At the time of the lawsuit, the supermax housed some 450 inmates, according to Raymond Vasvari, legal director of the Ohio ACLU.

Attorney Staughton Lynd, a well-known civil rights activist who directed the Mississippi Freedom Summer Project in the 1960s, is assisting in the lawsuit. He concedes that "some conditions have improved" since the lawsuit was filed, but the current hunger strike was prompted by six long-standing "major problems."

Prisoners' concerns include the procedures by which inmates are designated for supermax and released from it; the lack of an education and treatment plan for hepatitis C cases; the lack of hygiene products and access to postage and writing materials; the fact that "two-thirds of the supermax prisoners are black or Hispanic" and the prison refuses religious and cultural accommodations; the lack of any outdoor recreation program; and the fact that the prison's "mental health counseling program is conducted with the prisoner sitting on a concrete stool in a locked room, handcuffed behind his back and chained to the floor, and yelling to a counselor outside the cell," according to Lynd.

At a January 9 news conference, attorney Alice Lynd charged that prison officials use deliberate cruelty that goes beyond any legal sentence.

OSP and Ohio Department of Rehabilitation and Corrections spokespersons have declined comment thus far, citing the pending litigation.

Warden Todd Ishee has called the OSP inmates "the worst of the worst." He told the *Dayton Daily News* that prisoners are placed in the supermax after an administrative "due process hearing," because of assault on prison staff or other inmates, if they're gang leaders, or if they've tried to escape.

"There are four privilege levels, and inmates can work their way up through the levels—and eventually back to a less-secure prison—through good behavior and by participating in close-circuit television self-help programs," the *Daily News* reported.

Lynd contends that "a number of prisoners had been recommended for a decrease in security status [but] these recommendations by officials at the supermax, who are familiar with the prisoner, and his record at the facility are often vetoed" by corrections officials in Columbus.

Vasvari also denies there are any "meaningful hearings." He told the *Daily News*, "It's supposed to be for the worst of the worst, but it turns out you have some people there for minor rules infractions."

Other critics of the supermax—and some inmates—contend that prisoners are placed there for asserting their rights or offending a prison official. Lynd reports that at least one mentally disturbed inmate was transferred out of the supermax, but that medical and mental health care remains a concern. At the time of the lawsuit, Vasvari pointed to three suicides at the facility and denounced a "systematic deprivation of sensory stimuli, tailor-made to breed mental illness where it doesn't exist and exacerbate it where it does."

In their lawsuit, the prisoners declined to seek monetary damages, requesting instead a complete overhaul of the procedures used at the prison.

The so-called outdoor recreational program continues to come under fire; it consists of an empty cell with a graded slit in the wall to let in fresh air. It's this air flow from the "outside" that makes it officially an outdoor recreation area.

Many prisoners have complained that their cells are abnormally cold in winter and they're given fewer clothes and blankets to keep warm as a deliberate policy of cruelty. The Associated Press reported that inmates are shackled and strip-searched each time they leave their cell.

According to Lynd, there's currently no imam for Muslim prisoners, and Muslim prisoners who have special diet needs and request religious books and prayer apparatuses are neglected and ignored.

Lynd concedes that "the extent of the spreading hunger strike is difficult to determine," but says that inmate John Perotti "has consistently gone without food since the first of the month."

In a statement issued by Lynd, he noted, "I understand their frustration, a lawsuit takes a long time. When a prisoner cannot meet with other prisoners, cannot visit with reporters, cannot in most cases leave the prison to appear in person in court, he may come to feel that the only way he can call attention to his problem is to deprive himself of food. A fast is really a cry for help."

March 22, 2001

Snitch vs. Snitch

"**M**y name is Johnny WM. Byrd Jr., and I may very well be the next man murdered by the state of Ohio. I strongly use the word 'murder' and its complete definition, for if my execution is permitted to be carried out—it is nothing less!"

John Byrd wrote those words recently in a letter to Cleveland-area state Representative Shirley A. Smith. Byrd, who was sentenced to death for the murder of Cincinnati convenience store clerk Monte Tewksbury nearly 18 years ago, has steadfastly maintained his innocence while on Death Row. In 1994, he came within 30 minutes of being executed, before the Ohio Supreme Court granted him a last-minute reprieve. Now he hopes that previously ignored evidence of perjury will win him a new trial and spare his life.

A slew of affidavits gathered by the Ohio Public Defender's office suggest that while Byrd was at the crime scene in 1983, he was not the killer. The evidence includes two sworn statements from convicted accomplice John Brewer, who actually confessed it was he, not Byrd, who murdered Tewksbury.

Ohio Attorney General Betty Montgomery's office remains skeptical, though, questioning why it took so long for the affidavits to surface in the two-decades-old case.

And while the public defender's reliance on the word of cons and ex-cons raises doubts in the eyes of prosecutors, Byrd's attorneys point a finger back at them—Byrd was convicted through the testimony of a jailhouse informant Public Defender David Bodiker calls a "liar" and a "snitch."

Now the clock is ticking on Byrd's life. The final guaranteed appeal to stop his execution was denied by the U.S. Supreme Court on January 8, 2001. On March 20, the Ohio Supreme Court set Byrd's execution date for September 12 and, in the same decision, referred Byrd's persistent claim of actual innocence back to the Hamilton County Common Pleas Court for a hearing. With a hearing date yet to be set, the case is back in the county where the complicated drama Byrd calls a "nightmare" began.

During the afternoon and evening of April 17, 1983, John Byrd admits to consuming "large quantities of alcohol, barbiturates and marijuana," which caused him to black out. When he woke up the next day in A-Block of the Hamilton County Workhouse, he contends that he thought he was jailed on a drinking-related charge.

Rather, Byrd had been arrested in a van with two accomplices, John Brewer and William "Danny" Woodall, for the robbery of a Cincinnati King Kwik convenience store and the stabbing death of store clerk Monte Tewksbury, a Procter and Gamble employee who worked nights at the store. It was an unfortunate and unusual death—a single stab wound pierced his liver.

No direct physical evidence linked Byrd to Tewksbury's stabbing. Nevertheless, accomplices Woodall and Brewer were sentenced to life in prison and Byrd got the death penalty. Byrd's jury sentenced him to death primarily on the increasingly suspect testimony of a jailhouse snitch, Ronald Armstead, an inmate who claimed that Byrd confessed the murder to him. The *Cincinnati Enquirer* portrayed Armstead's testimony as dramatic and enthralling: "Observers in the packed courthouse appeared captivated by Armstead and a stunned silence fell over the courtroom."

Documents obtained by *Columbus Alive* shed new light on what happened the night of April 17 and the four subsequent months that Byrd spent in jail prior to his conviction on August 12, 1983.

More than five years after Byrd's conviction, Brewer signed a notarized affidavit substantiating Byrd's story. "I observed John Byrd Jr. drinking large quantities of beer and screwdrivers and taking narcotic drugs during the late afternoon and evening of April 17, 1983," Brewer stated. He described Byrd as "highly intoxicated" and recalled that Byrd "staggered as he walked into the store and was having a hard time standing up... John was so drunk and stoned that he leaned against the wall in the front of the store to stand up."

Brewer's sworn account of what happened next is as follows: "I ran to the front of the store where I leaped onto the front counter and then off the front counter in order to subdue the store clerk, Monte Tewksbury." Crime scene evidence revealed Brewer's footprint on the store's front counter.

Brewer, then described as an agile, five-feet, eight-inches tall and 135 pounds, claimed, "I grabbed Tewksbury by the arm and ordered him to give me all the money contained in the store's register." Tewksbury's autopsy listed bruises on his arm, possibly consistent with being forcibly grabbed.

Brewer said he "became distracted by lights which flashed through the front window in the store," creating the opportunity for the much heavier Tewksbury (approximately five-feet, six-inches, 240 pounds) to "grab" at Brewer.

"I reacted to Tewksbury's action by stabbing him," Brewer confessed in the 1989 affidavit.

He described the murder weapon as a "hunting knife with a five-inch, highly polished blade and bone handle." Brewer said that he later "threw the knife I used to stab Tewksbury out of the van." The police were never able to find the murder weapon, although during Byrd's trial the prosecutors dramatically waved around a work knife found in the van that allegedly belonged to Byrd, without ever attempting to establish it as the murder weapon.

On January 26, 2001, in a controversial and dramatic 11th-hour move, the Ohio Public Defender's Office released John Brewer's 1989 affidavit and submitted an updated affidavit dated January 24, 2001.

Brewer tells essentially the same tale, albeit in more colorful language, in the new, hand-written statement. He described John Byrd as "highly intoxicated and generally fucked up" during the evening of the murder. Brewer went into more detail about his confrontation with Tewksbury: "Tewksbury slung me to the side. I freed my left arm and got my knife from my waist and stabbed him in the side. I didn't think that he was seriously hurt because I did not see any blood."

"When I got back in the van, I said to Danny Woodall, 'Man, I stabbed a guy, take off,'" added Brewer.

Hamilton County Prosecutor Mike Allen dismissed Brewer's sworn confession. "What does he have to lose? It's a story a couple of convicted felons sitting around in their jail cells decided to concoct. It's worthless," he told the Associated Press.

Ohio Attorney General Betty Montgomery responded in writing to the Ohio Supreme Court by claiming that "Brewer now has nothing to lose. He cannot be sentenced to death for Monte Tewksbury's murder."

But, as the *Columbus Dispatch* reported prior to Montgomery's arguments to the state's highest court, "His [Brewer's] admission, if found to be true, could prevent his possible parole in 2015. In fact, Brewer had noted in his most recent affidavit that 'I am eligible for parole in 2015 and realize that I have a lot to lose by signing this affidavit,'" a detail ignored by Montgomery in her efforts to sustain Byrd's death sentence.

Still, the question of why the public defender's office would wait so long to release the 1989 affidavit remains. Public Defender David Bodiker said it has nothing to do with the merits of the claim. "I think that at the time I got it, there was an uncertainty how to use it," Bodiker said. "There was never a time where there was the ability to insert that claim [in court proceedings]. I feel that everybody here anticipated judicial relief for Mr. Byrd at some point."

The public defender's position has long been that Byrd should get a new trial, and the affidavit of actual innocence was viewed as a tactic of last resort that might save Byrd from the death penalty but wouldn't get him released from prison.

Timing is everything in death penalty cases. Had the public defender released the single Brewer affidavit more than a decade ago, it probably would have had very little impact, said some sources in the public defender's office.

Joe Case, spokesperson for Attorney General Montgomery, said the motion for actual innocence is based on "flimsy" evidence because it was held for more than a decade. "You would think that if they had information that could have gotten Mr. Byrd off of Death Row 12 years ago, they would have done it before now. In 1994, he was within hours of execution and the affidavit was never produced," Case said. "If there is credible information that could clear Mr. Byrd, that information should be laid on the table now and allow for the courts to decide."

"The attorney general sees this as nothing more than delay tactics to buy time for a man who has gone all the way through the system. He has exhausted all of his appeals and now they are grasping at straws to delay the inevitable," Case continued. "We will strongly oppose introduction of new evidence because what the court ordered was a hearing and ruling on the specific actual innocence claim that has been brought forward here."

When asked how the attorney general's office could both want the public defender to come forward with evidence, but oppose the introduction of new evidence, Case clarified: "If they have evidence that would clear their man, then it needs to be dealt with through the proper channels. We can't be asking the trial court on this level to go beyond its orders from the Supreme Court and deal with the Brewer affidavit."

Ohio Supreme Court Chief Justice Thomas Moyer said it will be up to the Hamilton County Common Pleas Court judge to decide which evidence will be admissible at the hearing. "I would think it would be an evidentiary hearing limited to that issue," he told *Columbus Alive*.

Earlier this year, *Columbus Alive* contacted Prison Advocacy Network activist Dan Cahill about the Byrd case. A 24-year veteran of Ohio prisons who was incarcerated for drug trafficking, aggravated robbery and burglary, Cahill said he served time in prisons where John Brewer, John Byrd and Danny Woodall were inmates, and that all three confirmed that it was Brewer, not Byrd, who killed Tewksbury.

Cahill later went public with his story, and the Ohio Public Defender's office recently obtained a notarized affidavit from Cahill that supports Byrd's claims.

While at the Southern Ohio Correctional Facility in the mid-1980s, Cahill, a Death Row porter, met Byrd. The convicted Death Row inmate "adamantly" maintained his innocence, Cahill said. He claimed Byrd told him "he was really drunk at the time."

Cahill swore that Brewer "said he was the one who killed the guy... [and he] also said that Byrd was really messed up at the time of the crime." Cahill later met Woodall at Orient Correctional Institute and swears that "Woodall told me that Brewer did the killing... He just said they got the wrong one on Death Row."

With the release of the new affidavits this year, and with media scrutiny on the Byrd case mounting, the attorney general's office and Hamilton County prosecutors dispatched State Trooper Howard Hudson and Special Prosecutor Mark Piepmeier to see Woodall in order to get him to sign an affidavit implicating Byrd. While the pair could not produce a signed affidavit from Woodall, Hudson and Piepmeier provided their own affidavits, based on January 29 and January 31 visits at London Correctional Institution and the Ohio State University

Hospital respectively, claiming the terminally ill Woodall told them Byrd did it.

Woodall told Hudson and Piepmeier that in 1989, Brewer asked him to conspire with Brewer to clear Byrd, according to attorney general spokesperson Case. "So we have evidence that even back in 1989, we have another co-defendant saying that he was asked by Mr. Brewer to concoct a lie to clear Mr. Byrd," Case said.

Although the Hudson and Piepmeier affidavits are of little value as evidence in court, they may publicly strengthen the case of Montgomery and Hamilton County prosecutors. According to attorneys in the public defender's office, Hudson and Piepmeier are high-profile witnesses who lend credibility to the case against Byrd. Both men played key roles in the investigation into the April 1993 Lucasville prison riot; Hudson was an on-scene negotiator and post-riot investigator; Piepmeier was a special prosecutor who convicted the rioting inmates.

When the public defender's office requested access to Woodall to discuss the Byrd case, according to attorneys in the office, prison officials said Woodall was not available and, because he is suffering from cancer, had a tube down his throat. Prison sources reported that a day after Piepmeier, Hudson and Hamilton County Prosecutor William Breyer first visited Woodall in prison, Woodall was transferred to OSU Hospital.

John Brewer's most recent affidavit also addresses John Byrd's alleged jailhouse confession. "At our initial appearance on this case in Municipal Court, my attorney Mr. Blackmore advised all three of us not to talk about the case with anybody. I would not talk to a black guy about anything serious. That is ridiculous that I would talk to a black guy about a serious matter," Brewer wrote in reference to informant Ronald Armstead, who is black.

Additional affidavits obtained during the *Columbus Alive* investigation call into question the truthfulness of Armstead's key testimony. Denver Nicely Jr., a friend of Byrd's father, was in A-Block of the Hamilton County jail in the spring of 1983. He swears there was no way that Byrd talked to Armstead because, "At the time John Byrd Jr. and I did not like black people. We did not talk with black people about anything. Ronald Armstead, Marvin Randolph and Vernon Jordan are black." The three inmates mentioned by Nicely had reputations as jailhouse snitches.

Another black inmate, Lester Early, confirms in a sworn affidavit, "It was known by everyone in A-Block that Armstead, Jordan and others were out to get Byrd to get themselves some play on their cases... Byrd kept to himself. He and his co-defendants were new guys on A-Block. Byrd did not go around running his mouth about his case."

Moreover, Early dismisses Armstead's trial testimony alleging that Byrd confessed to him on May 26, 1983, while the two were watching a TV show portraying the tragic death of Tewksbury and showing home video of the happy Tewksbury family. Since Byrd supposedly confessed during the TV show, the jury was able to watch the heart-wrenching family videotape under the guise of "evidence."

"There was only one television in A-Block. I never heard Byrd say anything about his case while watching television. I never had anyone say they heard Byrd say anything about his case," Early said. Early also claims that police and Hamilton County prosecutors regularly talked with the three snitches under the pretext that they were going to court.

Keith Wieland, who was also serving time in the jail, says that the three snitches met with him, and that Randolph said, "I have a great idea on how to get us out of our separate problems."

"'Bull' [Armstead] suggested that we say we overheard or we were told by John Byrd Jr. and his co-defendants that they had committed this murder/robbery. I was approached specifically by 'Bull' because he and the other individuals were black and I was white. 'Bull' stated that it would be more believable that three white guys would talk to another white person, not just four black guys," Wieland said.

Wieland turned them down. His affidavit states that the three snitches then wrote a letter to the Hamilton County Prosecutor's office anyway, and drew attention to themselves by discussing how to spell Prosecutor Arthur M. Ney Jr.'s last name.

Two other affidavits, from inmates Abdul Mughni and Robert Ashbrook, both cast doubt on the likelihood of a Byrd confession to Armstead. Mughni's affidavit noted, "I never saw John Byrd speak with Ronald Armstead or Vernon Jordan. Generally, blacks and whites did not want to be seen associating with each other... After Armstead and Jordan testified, I overheard them bragging about what they had done. Armstead and Jordan said they were going to be back on the street soon because of the deals they got for testifying against Byrd, Brewer and Woodall."

Ashbrook asserted, "John Byrd did not go around the workhouse talking about his case. In 1983 in the workhouse blacks and whites did not associate with each other."

As reported by *Columbus Alive* in August 2000, Armstead's crucial testimony—where a weeping Armstead portrayed Byrd as a calculated, cold-blooded killer—raises concern. Armstead failed to tell the jury that he faced up to 15 years in prison for a parole violation and escaping from jail after assaulting a nurse in the sick ward and beating a guard with a metal bed crank. Armstead portrayed to the jury that he had no jail time pending and was testifying as part of his civic duty. The Hamilton County prosecutors vouched for Armstead's testimony and failed to disclose his incorrect and possibly perjured testimony regarding the sentence hanging over his head.

Daniel J. Breyer, the Hamilton County prosecutor who prosecuted the Byrd case, sent a letter to the parole board praising Armstead's cooperation in the case. As the *Columbus Dispatch* reported, "A few hours later, Armstead was on a plane headed to San Diego," despite the initial adamant objections of the parole board.

During proceedings away from the jury in Byrd's original trial, Byrd attorney Hollis Moore raised concerns about the disclosure of Armstead's criminal past. Byrd's trial judge, Donald Schott, said, "It is within the sound discretion of the court as to the extent of the exploration of the criminal records." The judge continued, "I did not feel that it was necessary that we go into them unless it was something that touched upon the area of perjury."

Byrd's attorneys believe Armstead may have perjured himself when asked if he had any charges pending against him. The star witness testified, "I don't have no time pending or nothing else pending… I don't have no more cases pending and I come to testify against Byrd because he was wrong."

The defense tried to ask Armstead to divulge information about his criminal past no fewer than five times. First the defense attorney asked if he was serving time and for what charges. The prosecutors objected to this question and the judge sustained the objection. The defense asked if Armstead was convicted of a federal or state offense or had served more than a year in prison. The judge again sustained the prosecutors' objection. The interrogation continued as such until Armstead made the infamous claim that he had "no time pending."

Hamilton County attorney Fred Hoefle, who represented Byrd on appeal, failed to raise the issue on appeal—a mistake, said Public Defender David Bodiker. "First of all, they didn't get into what a culprit Armstead was."

In April 2000, Sixth Circuit Court Judge Nathaniel R. Jones stated, "At best, these [Armstead's] statements were misleading and left the jury with a material mis-impression of fact. At worst, these statements were patently false, which the prosecution knew, or should have known." Jones dissented from the two-judge majority in the appeals court ruling, which upheld Byrd's conviction.

A comparison of the Woodall, Brewer and Byrd murder trials reveals differences in the way Armstead was presented as a witness. In Brewer's trial, Armstead testified that Brewer said things strikingly similar to what Byrd supposedly said. Armstead told the jury that Byrd confessed: "Fuck him [Tewksbury], he deserved to die." Armstead told another jury that Brewer confessed: "Fuck him. He need to be dead."

In the Byrd trial, Armstead testified that prison guards were present when Byrd was said to have confessed to the crime. No guards testified to back up this claim.

In Woodall's case, Armstead admitted that he was serving six months for assault. In Brewer's case, Armstead admitted to the court, "I had a trafficking case I went to the penitentiary on, and felonious assault that I went to the penitentiary on."

But in Byrd's case, the jury had no idea that Armstead was in jail on a parole violation and faced a possible return to state prison. "What they did do, of course, was allow misconceptions about his record go to the jury unchallenged," Bodiker said.

Of Armstead's testimony, Joe Case countered, "That issue has been looked at and scrutinized by numerous levels of judicial review and it has been upheld."

As for concerns about the jury being unaware of Armstead's pending sentence, the attorney general's spokesperson continued, "For them to say that they did not have a venue to present this at this point is surprising, given the creativity demonstrated by the public defender's office in the past."

As it turns out, Hamilton County's star witness, with a long criminal history in Ohio, has been less than a good citizen since the Byrd trial. Armstead now drifts between Las Vegas and San Diego. Court records indicate he has at least two Social Security numbers and has been charged with various crimes.

Las Vegas Township court records list a 1990 felony assault and drug trafficking conviction for Armstead. His rap sheet also shows a 1991 battery with a deadly weapon charge, an obstructing a police officer charge, a resisting arrest charge, and a 1994 citation for battery.

An October 24, 1995, police report states that Armstead attacked a highly intoxicated individual and left "the victim bleeding from his nose" and with blood all over his jacket. Armstead was charged with strong armed robbery for allegedly stealing $145 from the individual. Charges were later dropped when the victim refused to testify against Armstead.

On December 11, 1996, a Las Vegas Township police report alleged that Armstead robbed a woman of $12,000 in jewelry by "grab[bing] her around the neck." He was charged with a felony count of robbery and resisting arrest. The victim, who resides in New York, failed to return and testify against Armstead and the charges were dropped.

Prison records indicate that Armstead is of "below average" intelligence with an IQ between 80 and 89 and a long history of violence and drug addiction.

Those in the Ohio Public Defender's office familiar with the Byrd case are struck by Hamilton County's pursuit and defense of the Death Row conviction. Sure, prosecutors are there to seek convictions for the criminally indicted, and public defenders try to get their clients off the hook, or at least a reduced sentence, but something about the Byrd case is remarkable, they say.

"They tried everything," Public Defender David Bodiker said. "When they're questioned, they try to do a lot of things."

William Breyer, who's responsible for prosecuting Byrd's post-conviction appeals and bringing about his execution (and who's also the brother of original trial prosecutor Daniel Breyer), even sued Byrd and the Public Defender's office in 1990, demanding attorney's fees at the rate of $75 an hour for having to defend against Byrd's legal claims of innocence. He lost.

William Breyer also wrote the Director of the Ohio Prosecuting Attorneys Association and the Ohio Public Defender's office accusing Byrd's post-conviction attorney, Richard Vickers, of misconduct. The public defender's office says Vickers was trying to locate a victim impact statement in which Tewksbury's widow Sharon said Byrd told her he wanted to know what murder "felt like"; prosecutors claimed Vickers should have contacted them before retrieving the statement.

A call to Breyer seeking comment was forwarded to John Ester, spokesperson for the Hamilton County Prosecutor's office; Ester did not return a telephone message for the sake of this story.

Attorneys in the public defender's office also believe Attorney General Betty Montgomery and the Hamilton County Prosecutor's office continue to insist on Byrd's guilt because of what it says about the death penalty in general. If Byrd is not guilty of the crime that sent him to Death Row, then the system in Ohio, just like elsewhere, is imperfect, makes mistakes, and sometimes might kill the wrong person.

The attorney general's office remains steadfast that justice was upheld. "We'll be there and we'll vigorously defend our position," spokesperson Joe Case said of the pending Byrd hearing.

Byrd, while lobbying for his innocence and his life, said he does feel sorry for Sharon Tewksbury, who has made statements to the press supporting Byrd's death sentence. "I have sympathy for Ms. Tewksbury," Byrd wrote in a

February 3, 2001, letter to *Columbus Alive.* "She lost her husband. She has also been used and manipulated by the prosecutor's office to no end."

For Bodiker, the case boils down to one simple fact: Another man has confessed to the murder for which John Byrd is to be executed. "The bottom line for us is, John Brewer said 'I did it.' He continues to say 'I did it.'"

Co-written with Jamie Pietras
March 29, 2001

Judicious Procedures

Executing people pays off politically. State Treasurer Joe Deters knows this. He's parlayed his "kill at any cost" rent-a-snitch approach in Hamilton County into a recent announcement that he wants to replace the legendary Bloody Mama herself, current Attorney General Betty Montgomery.

Governor Bob Taft, meanwhile, is too busy conjuring up the spirit of Richard Nixon—invoking "executive privilege" to prevent scrutiny of secret backroom meetings concerning the state's budget—to be bothered with life-or-death questions about justice.

This leaves, perhaps, Ohio Supreme Court Chief Justice Thomas J. Moyer as the lone voice of sanity suggesting, despite campaign plans by his Republican cohorts, that we should proceed judiciously when it comes to state-sanctioned murder.

Before the state kills Jay D. Scott, we ought to consider that information about his well-documented mental illness was withheld from the jury that condemned him to death. But it wasn't withheld from the prison guards who routinely brutalize him, as they do other mentally ill inmates in Ohio's prison system, according to a 13-year-old report from six Ohio inmates.

In perusing my Scott file, after he was within an hour of

being killed last Tuesday, I came across a complaint filed by Scott and five other Lucasville inmates dated June 17, 1988. The complaint is titled "Regarding human rights violations at the Southern Ohio Correctional Facility" and it's addressed to Amnesty International. The document is a savage indictment of the Ohio prison system—not that any statewide politicians would care.

Scott and others—and I believe they are far closer to the truth than the Ma Montgomery Gang running the state—complained that they were "being systematically victimized by some of the most barbaric and inhumane methods ever devised by man." The inmates wrote, "Men are being literally tortured by Ohio prison officials."

But isn't that what prisons are for in the post-Reagan Reich? The inmates' long list of abuse allegations are captured in 31 pages of fascinating reading.

As part of the rehabilitation process, "Prisoners in J1 Supermax are subjected to routine 'strip searches' before leaving their cell for any reason and before being put back in the cell. A 'strip search' consists of forcing the prisoner to get naked, open his mouth and pull his lips down, run his fingers through his hair, lift his arms, raise his penis and testicles and skin his penis back, then turn around and show the bottom of his feet one at a time, and then bend over and spread the cheeks of his buttocks. This practice is often accompanied by sexual comments from guards and is degrading and humiliating," the inmates wrote.

This no doubt improved the mental health of Scott, who was first incarcerated at age nine and had spent nearly a decade in adult prison prior to killing Vinney Prince in 1983.

The inmates' report documents in detail the standard practices at Lucasville: the chainings, the use of "high-pressure fire hoses," the rampant and capricious use of "chemical mace and tear gas," the sleeping on concrete floors, and brutal beatings by "sadistic guards." All of this should be old news to those who have studied the Ohio prison system and are familiar with the Lucasville riots.

A section of the complaint that caught my attention is called "Prisoners who are mentally ill are placed in J1 because of their mental illness." It begins: "Ohio prison officials frequently place prisoners who are mentally ill [and] under psychiatric care or who have long histories of mental problems in J1 Supermax for behavior which is a product of the mental illness."

Scott, for example, with his long history of abuse and schizophrenia, could be better tortured prior to his politically celebrated murder.

The prisoners documented how Cornellius Pernel, confined to a Mississippi State Psychiatric Hospital when he was 10 years old, was beaten by Lucasville guards in 1987. After the beating, the guards had him transferred to the J1 Supermax where, despite ingesting "powerful psychotropic drugs four times each day," he managed to cut his wrists and rant and rave endlessly while throwing feces and urine at the guards "for no reason."

The complaint documents the case of Alonzo Taylor, who was confined in various mental institutions between the ages of nine and 20 as a result of being forced to perform oral sex on his father. As part of his therapy at Lucasville, the complaint alleged, the guards placed a "restraining belt around his wrists and pulled him backwards to the first flight of stairs where he fell down." The guards then provided incentive for Taylor to walk back up by beating and kicking him.

Hank Rimmers received similar treatment as a mentally ill inmate when "a guard broke his wrist and arm with a billy club." The inmates in their complaint likened Lucasville to the Nazi camps "Treblinka and Dachau."

Another part of the complaint well worth reading involves mentally ill patients in two other sections of the prison who were allegedly abused by guards. The case of James Richards is illustrative. He was found dead in his cell on November 4, 1987. Richards, a manic-depressive with suicidal tendencies, never received the treatment required to keep him sane and, with little supervision, "ingested a fatal dose of his own, and others,' medication."

I've been writing a song with my friend Ed, called "The Bob Taft Death House Blues," in honor of a skilled politician who managed to pop out of the right womb with the right name. We're still working on it, but so far we've got a few lines down:

> His granddaddy was fat
> His morals are thin
> If you're on Death Row
> He'll do you in.
> If you're retarded
> He's real cold-hearted
> Mentally ill?
> He's still got to kill.
> If you're a juvenile
> He's in denial.
> Like Bonnie and Clyde
> He's got a Bloody Mama

Right by his side.
Betty's her name
Murder's her fame.
And they won't stop killin'
Unless the voters make them lose—
We've got the Bob Taft death house blues...

April 26, 2001

Death vs. Life
(Sentence)

Jay D. Scott might not have been sent to Death Row
had his jury been properly informed of the law, according to statements obtained by Scott's attorneys. A fifth
juror who sentenced Scott to death is now questioning the
fairness of that verdict, and he claims that Scott may have
received life in prison had the jury been aware of that
option.

"I wish we could go back in time and be informed of
what we needed to know at Mr. Scott's sentencing. We
would have come up with a different result—I'm sure of
it," said juror John Patten in a statement released by Scott's
attorney, John Pyle, on May 11, 2001, four days before
Scott's scheduled execution.

Scott was convicted of the 1983 murder of 74-year-old
Cleveland delicatessen owner Vinney Prince. Scott was to
be executed on May 15—his third scheduled date with
death—despite protestations from his attorney that, as a
diagnosed schizophrenic, Scott was unfit to understand the
punishment. The U.S. Circuit Court of Appeals stopped
Tuesday's execution three minutes before Scott was to be
killed so the court can review the case.

Pyle charges that Scott "grew up in a nightmare that his

jurors never learned about at trial." He cites Scott's "horrific childhood and the unimaginable suffering he experienced at the hands of abusive, alcoholic and drug-dependent parents."

While there's little doubt that Scott is afflicted with serious mental illness, Pyle raises the question of whether or not Scott "may also have been suffering from some degree of mental illness at the time of trial." Under Ohio law, Scott's present mental illness is not a factor in his execution as long as he's aware that he's being killed for a crime he committed.

"As it was, we [the jury] were not aware of what we needed to know to make a good decision," Patten said. "Mr. Scott was represented by appointed attorneys who were not well prepared. The picture we were left with was that Jay D. Scott was as bad a person as you could find."

Patten claims, "All of us [jurors] were called into the trial judge's chambers right after it was all over and told that Jay D. Scott was a career criminal. We were also told about his being guilty of another murder that had occurred around the same time as the one in our case. So any juror who recently signed a declaration was aware of this."

In his April 10 statement denying clemency for Scott, Ohio Governor Bob Taft concluded, "There is no indication that the jurors, from whom Scott's attorneys obtained statements, were told about Mr. Scott's prior violent criminal behavior or asked how such information may have impacted their decision."

Five Scott jurors have signed a sworn declaration saying that they have "grave doubts" about executing Scott.

On March 31, juror Verlene S. Estremera stated: "I find it troubling that the defense attorneys failed to represent any mitigating or extenuating circumstances regarding Mr. Scott and his life and background. I now understand that there was information about Mr. Scott's upbringing that was not presented to us that would have been useful to know; it would have been useful as a juror to know, for example, that Mr. Scott grew up in circumstances of neglect, abuse and severe poverty, and that he was exposed to extreme violence as a child; it would have been very useful to know that he suffered from a history of mental illness as serious as schizophrenia."

Estremera said that she couldn't speak for the other jurors, but "had I known this information, it would have made a difference with respect to Mr. Scott's sentence."

Patten also claims that he seriously misunderstood Ohio law, as did the rest of the jury, which would allow one juror to veto the death sentence and move on to consider life in prison as an alternative.

Patten alleged that there was a "holdout juror in Scott's case during the sentencing."

"It was clear that this juror did not want to vote for a death sentence. She felt a lot of pressure to change her vote, and probably ultimately gave in only because she thought that if she couldn't convince anyone else to change their vote, that she had to change hers. Had we known that under the law her holding out did not mean we would be a hung jury, but instead meant we were then to consider the alternative life sentences before us, we would have ended up with a life sentence for Mr. Scott. I'm sure of it," Patten said.

Juror Bernice Williams also alleges that the jurors did not adequately understand the law at the time of Scott's sentencing. In a March 27 statement, she asserted, "I find it troubling to be informed that the law in Ohio is such that in a death penalty case the vote of a single juror is sufficient to prevent a death sentence; we were not instructed of this and I did not understand this."

Scott's attorneys' appeals claimed that their client's execution would be a violation of the Eighth Amendment prohibition against "cruel and unusual punishment," and that the "evolving standards" of justice in the U.S. bar the execution of the mentally ill. If Scott is executed, despite jurors' admissions that they did not understand the law when they sentenced him to death, it will prove just how fickle those standards are.

May 17, 2001

Rogue State

As *Columbus Alive* goes to press, Jay D. Scott is scheduled to die for the third—and perhaps final—time this year, on June 14, 2001. Scott's two unprecedented stays of execution raise a host of questions about how the death penalty is implemented in the Buckeye State.

Although overshadowed by the execution of Oklahoma City bomber Timothy McVeigh, Scott's lengthy history on Death Row calls critical attention to the issue of executing the mentally ill.

Ohio Supreme Court Justice Paul Pfeiffer's May 11, 2001, dissent in the Scott case contained some of the most eloquent prose in recent memory: "The Ohio Constitution is the product of Ohio, an enlightened, progressive state. When Ohioans consider the countries that still practice slavery, we call them uncivilized; when Ohioans consider the countries who do not permit women to vote, we call them repressive; when Ohioans consider the countries that permit state-sponsored torture, we call them barbaric."

"Jay D. Scott is in no other way a sympathetic man. He is a twice-convicted murderer who does not appear to express remorse for his crimes. But I cannot get past one simple irrefutable fact: He has chronic, undifferentiated schizophrenia, a severe mental illness," Pfeiffer pointed out.

"As a society, we have always treated those with mental illness differently from those without. In the interest of human dignity, we must continue to do so."

Americans who can't understand why the U.S. was removed from the United Nations' Human Rights Committee should know that international human rights standards condemn the execution of both the mentally retarded and the mentally ill. The small handful of nations that blatantly violate this standard are perceived as "rogue" nations. The U.N. Commission on Human Rights adopted a resolution urging all nations that retain the death penalty not to use it "on a person suffering from any form of mental disorder."

As Pfeiffer noted, "Executing Jay D. Scott says more about our society than it says about him. Executing him will be another assertion of our country's place in the world with China, Congo, Iran and Saudi Arabia as the five countries that year after year perform the most state-sanctioned executions. Executing him will be another assertion that taking the life of someone with mental illness is no different than taking the life of someone without mental illness. Executing him will be an assertion that taking the life of someone with mental illness serves a purpose that keeping him securely in prison for the rest of his life does not. Executing him will be an assertion that only some life is precious or sacred. I believe Ohioans are better than that."

Scott was convicted and sentenced to death for the 1983 murder of Vinney Prince, a Cleveland delicatessen owner. During his trial, Scott's attorneys decided not to offer mitigating evidence about his well-documented history of mental illness.

Nor did they disclose evidence concerning the violent and harsh world in which Scott was raised and lived. His father nearly stabbed his mother to death in front of the children. Both a brother and a sister were fatally shot. Another brother was shot and paralyzed and an older sister died in a house fire prior to Scott's birth.

Scott's attorneys gambled that withholding the evidence of his wretched life would make the jury less likely to find him guilty and condemn him to death. The strategy backfired when the jury took only 15 minutes to reach a guilty verdict.

Anti-death penalty activists, and Scott's post-conviction attorneys, argue that the misguided strategy essentially denied Scott his right to effective counsel. The U.S. Sixth Circuit Court of Appeals, while conceding that this claim concerning effective counsel constituted a "close call," concluded that Scott could only produce evidence of a "hypothetical juror" who might have voted differently had he heard the mitigating evidence during the death penalty phase.

As *Alive* reported last month, five actual Scott case jurors have signed sworn statements saying that the evidence may have made a difference in their sentencing—and two jurors say they would have voted for life in prison, not the death penalty, had they heard the withheld evidence. Under Ohio law, only one trial juror voting for a life sentence can stop the death penalty.

Michael Manley, spokesperson for Ohioans to Stop Executions, said, "Evolving standards of decency may mandate a whole new judicial approach to all who suffer from severe mental impairments, and certainly the defense should ask the courts to look at Mr. Scott's history of mental illness in light of evolving standards, and the courts should feel free to take a look and issue a stay for a third time to give them time to do so."

On April 17, 2001, the Ohio Supreme Court issued the first stay only an hour before Scott's scheduled execution. On May 15, with shunts already in his arms so there would be no problem finding a vein for lethal injection, Scott's execution was stayed at 8:57 p.m.—three minutes before his scheduled death.

Barring a third miracle, Ohioans may be left with Justice Pfeiffer's cry from the moral wilderness: "In this case, there is no doubt about the mental illness; the trial court found that Jay D. Scott has schizophrenia, a severe mental illness. I cannot sanction this execution. I dissent."

June 14, 2001

They Don't Want Him To Fry

Ohio prison Director Reginald A. Wilkinson yearns for John W. Byrd Jr. to go quietly into the dark abyss of death by lethal injection. Wilkinson, Governor Bob Taft and Attorney General Betty Montgomery want Byrd to roll over and play—I mean, *be*—dead.

Wilkinson announced last week that he wants a moratorium on using Old Sparky, Ohio's official electric chair; a bill pending in the Statehouse would also end electrocution as one of two ways Ohio kills its Death Row convicts.

Byrd wants to die in the electric chair with no hood covering his face—basically, he wants his execution to be as gruesome and public as possible, and to stare his accusers in the eyes as his flesh fries. But the captains of the death penalty are scrambling to take that choice away from him before Byrd's scheduled September 12, 2001, execution.

They hope to obscure the fact that they're killing a man without any direct evidence against him, other than the word of a felon and a jailhouse snitch working on behalf of the Hamilton County prosecutors. They're killing the wrong man and he refuses to cooperate.

Montgomery and Taft have always preferred to execute those who don't fight back, like a documented mentally retarded volunteer. The hypocrisy of the right-wing Republican crowd is staggering as they joyously suck up to the Christian Right and wear their WWJD bracelets while forgetting the Ten Commandments.

I absolutely support Byrd's choice of death by the electric chair with no hood. Byrd recently told me that, if the execution is carried out, he hopes his death "helps to bring down this barbaric system, brings down the pillars in the temple."

"They want to ignore the fact that the first two guys who basically surrendered were paralyzed by drugs and then suffocated," Byrd said, referring to first two executed in Ohio since the reinstatement of the death penalty, Wilford Berry and Jay D. Scott, who died by lethal injection. "I'm not going to surrender to this." Nor should he.

Byrd has been on Death Row since he was 18 years old. He's now 37.

On April 18, 1983, Byrd woke up in a Hamilton County jail thinking he'd been arrested for public intoxication. He was alone in a cell when law enforcement officers told him he was incarcerated for murder. They asked him to "roll over" on the two guys he'd been riding around with in the van the night before—John Brewer and William Woodall. Byrd refused, saying he had blacked out and didn't know a murder had taken place. He couldn't recall any of the details from his booze- and drug-filled night.

The only direct evidence the state could muster against Byrd was the testimony of jailhouse snitch Ronald Armstead, a black man, who claimed that Byrd, a white man, had confessed to him in the Cincinnati jail—not a likely scenario in a mostly racially divided jail in one of the U.S.'s most racially divided cities. Armstead perjured himself on the stand by failing to tell the jury he was in jail on a parole violation after violently beating a nurse and a prison guard and that he was facing up to 15 years in prison. The Hamilton County prosecutor vouched for Armstead's character.

Armstead, who had a long career of criminal convictions, made the absurd claim that he was simply doing his duty and testifying as a good citizen—a lie of monumental proportion, that the prosecution let stand before the jury. Armstead later acknowledged he had a deal with the prosecution, which freed him soon after the trial. This was curious, since the same prosecutor's office had vehemently opposed Armstead's parole the year before, citing evidence that he was a career criminal with prior convictions for sodomy, assault and drug offenses. Armstead is now in Las Vegas, where he was charged with robberies in 1995 and 1999.

Since the mid-1980s, Brewer has been telling fellow prisoners that they've got the wrong man on Death Row. He first signed an affidavit in 1989 admitting that he killed Tewksbury. He reaffirmed that affidavit just this year. Attorney General Betty Montgomery will tell you that Brewer had nothing to lose by signing the affidavit. That's a lie. By signing the affidavit, Brewer sacrificed any chance that he might be released on parole.

Another standard lie Montgomery's peddling is that "over 50 judges" had reviewed Byrd's case. The fact is, Byrd has been asking judges to grant him an evidentiary hearing since 1988 so he could present his evidence and witnesses to prove that he didn't kill Tewksbury. Not one judge has ever allowed Byrd to present his evidence in court with a hearing as to his actual claim of innocence.

Don't believe Montgomery and Taft's politically motivated assurance that it couldn't happen, that an innocent man couldn't be convicted in Ohio. Between 1927 and 1986, the state of Ohio released six men who had been condemned to death for murder, based on evidence of actual innocence. Add another 12 innocent men who were released after being convicted of murder, without death penalty specifications. This averages one innocent man being released every four years during that 60-year period.

Montgomery and Taft want Byrd to die quietly because the facts surrounding his death penalty conviction are so unsettling.

July 26, 2001

The Man In The Plaid Shirt?

Sources close to the John Byrd case have long specu-
lated about the possibility of an unknown fourth
man involved in the robberies on the night Monte
Tewksbury was murdered. Documents obtained by
Columbus Alive this week lend serious credibility to that theory for the first time, just 13 days before Byrd is to be executed for a crime he insists he did not commit.

Columbus Alive obtained two handwritten notes from the
sheriff's investigation file apparently written by a snitch.
The notes concern a tip on one Robert Pottinger—who
was 17 at the time of the Tewksbury murder—who rode in
the van with Byrd and his accomplices the day they
allegedly robbed the King Kwik and U-Tote-M stores and
who said he was told he faced murder charges in the
Tewksbury slaying.

Robert Pottinger admitted to *Columbus Alive* this week
that he was in the van with John Byrd, John Brewer and
William "Danny" Woodall. But when asked when he was
dropped off—before or after the robberies—Pottinger
repeatedly said, "I don't know," before adding, "The questions you're asking me are kinda incriminating."

The first document obtained by *Alive* is dated April 23,

1983, and is carbon-copied to a Cincinnati police officer. The note reads: "Let him off between two robberies Pottinger was with them when they pulled King Kwik Robbery. May have been wearing plaid shirt." The first note also states that Pottinger had been "Gone since Wednesday."

The second note, dated the next day, refers to a "Murder" weapon described as: "BLK. Handle," "Rusty and Back at Hilt—Silver Hand Guard (Hilt)," "FT. Long-Rust on Blade By Handle."

The note closes with these words: "Heard Bobby involved, Split Town, Always Wears Plaid Shirts."

In Monte Tewksbury's dying declaration to customer Cecil Conley, he described the individual who stabbed him as wearing a "plaid" shirt. Prosecution documents also refer to a "checked" shirt as the attire worn by Tewksbury's murderer. The man with the knife at the U-Tote-M robbery later that night was described as wearing "tan pants" and a "red and black jacket."

When Byrd, Brewer and Woodall were arrested at approximately 1 a.m. on April 18, 1983, inside a red work truck, Byrd was wearing "blue slacks" and a sweater with wide blue, yellow and black stripes.

Throughout post-conviction proceedings, the Ohio Public Defender's office has stressed that Brewer was "not wearing either a jacket or a shirt at the time of his arrest. Instead he was wearing only a thin T-shirt and remarked to the arresting officer concerning how cold he was on this early spring morning."

Brewer had on blue jeans. Woodall had on a blue sweater and blue jeans. Since Byrd's clothes failed to match eyewitness identification from either robbery, the prosecutors had to fall back on excuses about the stress the witnesses were under, which may have led to the mistaken clothing identification.

Pottinger could not recall whether he or any of the three accomplices wore a plaid shirt on the night of the murder. "I don't know. It was kind of chilly outside," he told *Alive*. "I couldn't tell you what I was wearing that night. I don't remember that."

The reference in the snitch's note to a foot-long knife is consistent with Tewksbury's dying statement that he was stabbed with "the biggest goddamn knife I've ever seen." While the prosecutors waved a six-inch knife around at Byrd's trial to mesmerize the jury, they conceded that it was neither the murder weapon in the King Kwik robbery nor did it match the knife marks on a door at the later U-Tote-M robbery.

When asked about the missing murder weapon by *Alive*, Pottinger said, "I never saw a knife that night. When we did robberies, we didn't use weapons. We didn't need them."

Public records from the Byrd case reveal that Pottinger should have been taken seriously as a suspect in the robberies. Hamilton County Sheriff's Detectives James Dattilo and Thomas Simmons interviewed Pottinger on May 6, 1983. Pottinger admitted that he began drinking and smoking pot with Byrd about noon on April 17. He also told the detectives that Byrd and Brewer had split "a Quaalude and a half" that afternoon.

Pottinger also admitted to the police that he rode in the red truck with Byrd, Brewer and Woodall to Newport, Kentucky, and went to a place called Poopies where the 17-year-old split a couple of pints of Canadian Club with the trio. At 6 p.m. they crossed the bridge back into Cincinnati and went to Frank and Irene's Bar to drink and shoot pool.

The oddest part about Pottinger's May 6 testimony is that he claims to have left the pool hall in the red truck about 8:15 p.m. and "then they took me over to my house and ahh told me to get out and I asked em why. Then we got to arguing and they said that they had to take care of business and I said, 'Naw, that ain't good enough,' and he says ahh, 'Well we're facing a lot of time, Johnny Byrd did it,' and he said, 'Now get out,' and I got out of the van."

Pottinger claimed he heard this confession from an unnamed member of the trio three hours before the actual killing.

Pottinger claimed that Byrd owned a "Bowie Knife" and described it as "7-8 inches long." He also told police that Brewer said "I'm gonna have to kill somebody" and "We're facing a lot of time."

According to Pottinger, Brewer's confession also came prior to the robbery. Although in Pottinger's recollection they dropped him off at 8:15 p.m., the red truck was parked outside his house until "10:30." Pottinger denied to the police that he had any involvement in the King Kwik robbery, despite the fact that he admitted to being with Byrd from noon to 10:30 p.m.

After dropping Pottinger off, the trio proceeded to rob the King Kwik within 45 minutes, in Pottinger's version of the events.

When he testified at Brewer's trial on August 8, 1983, Pottinger admitted that between April and August that year he was an inmate at the Training Institute of Central Ohio (TICO), a juvenile detention facility, on a "robbery" charge.

He testified under oath that the trio in the red truck were at his house between 11:15 and 11:20 p.m., the approximate time of the murder a few miles away.

During his conversation with *Columbus Alive* this week, Pottinger offered an explanation for why his trial testimony and interrogation by police offers a disjointed timeline. "When they first questioned me, the police kinda tricked me," he said. "They would cut the tape recorder off and then they would discuss things." When the police would turn the recorder back on, "they would want it to go the way they wanted it."

"They had me up in TICO. They told me that charges were pending against me for murder," Pottinger continued. "I was young, and they tricked me into saying things that they wanted me to say."

At Byrd's trial, Pottinger admitted to the prosecutor that he "used the word 'kill' in the presence of John Byrd." He explained the reason for it as follows: "I told you that me and Johnny said we weren't going to let anybody mess with us." Pottinger also said that while Byrd had the Bowie knife, "he never carried it."

Pottinger said that after the trio robbed the King Kwik, they drove back to his house; so, by his own admissions, he was with the trio immediately before and immediately after the murder of Tewksbury.

Pottinger's height and weight, unlike Brewer's, was much closer to Byrd's in 1983. In 1987, Pottinger was convicted in Hamilton County of receiving stolen property and was placed on parole. He was convicted of robbery in 1989 and spent nearly 11 years in prison.

Why Pottinger was not pursued as a suspect in the Tewksbury case is still a mystery. Sources close to the case speculate that since he wasn't caught in the van, and he was a juvenile, it would have been nearly impossible to convict him.

Pottinger also doesn't know why he wasn't charged in the case, especially following the threats that he would be.

"I just don't see that there's going to be any justice done here," he told *Columbus Alive*. "You've got some of the most powerful people in Ohio wanting this to go through and they could care less that an innocent man's going to die."

Pottinger believes that John Brewer is Monte Tewksbury's real murderer. "He's the one that had all the blood on him," he said, though he added that he didn't see Brewer with blood on him but "heard" about it.

"I wish there was more I could do to help," added Pottinger, who was perhaps as close to the crime as anyone besides the three accomplices. "But I don't think they're even going to acknowledge it. They could care less what I say."

August 30, 2001

The Snitch

The state's star witness in Byrd's trial was a flamboy-ant jailhouse snitch, Ronald "Bull" Armstead. His extensive criminal record reveals that he was a hero-in user, pimp and violent felon. At trial, Armstead provid-ed the only direct evidence that Byrd killed Monte Tewksbury.

Armstead claims that, amid the racially divided atmos-phere in the Hamilton County Jail, the three white inmates, John Brewer, William Woodall and John Byrd, took the violent black felon into their confidence.

In a surreal stroke of fortune for the prosecution, Armstead just happened to be watching *PM Magazine* fea-turing the singing Tewksbury family performing the song they wrote for their dead father. Armstead testified that during the show, Brewer told him "Fuck him—he need to be dead," in reference to Tewksbury.

During the same show, Byrd supposedly told Armstead the very similar "Fuck him…he deserved to die." Armstead also claimed that Byrd blurted out a confession to him in Byrd's cell: "And he said, yeah, I killed him, I killed him, you know because he was in my muthafuckin' way, fuck him."

As a result of this alleged confession, dramatically recounted by Armstead while the *PM Magazine* tape of the singing Tewksburys played for the jury, Byrd was given a death sentence.

Armstead, facing up to 15 years in prison on a parole violation for beating a nurse and prison guard with a bed crank, lied to the jury about his impending prison time. The jailhouse informant told the jury, "I got about two more weeks before my time is up... I don't have no time pending or nothing else pending."

Instead of correcting this obvious misstatement, the prosecutor improperly vouched for Armstead's credibility. During closing arguments, Hamilton County prosecutors competed in extolling the virtues of Ronald Armstead. As one put it, "I believe Armstead when he took the stand and I...submit that you should believe him... Witnesses pay a price to testify... You know there's something real genuine about our people."

The Hamilton County Prosecutor's office, which had previously vehemently opposed Armstead's parole, quickly changed its mind and intervened to have him released from prison shortly after he testified.

Armstead was released two months after he testified at Byrd's trial and immediately flew to San Diego to live with his brother. The prosecutors originally claimed that Armstead's brother paid for the flight, however Armstead's brother is on record saying the he didn't pay for the plane ticket; he knew nothing about his brother's release until about a week before when he was contacted by either the Adult Parole Authority or the prosecutor's office and informed that Armstead was being released and would be flying to San Diego.

Martin Yant, an investigative reporter and private investigator hired by the Columbus Institute for Contemporary

Journalism, contacted Armstead's relatives last week; they claimed Armstead is now working for an Alaskan cruise line and is spending most of his time offshore. Armstead could not be reached for comment.

Hamilton County prosecutors have adamantly denied that they cut any deal with Armstead in exchange for his testimony. Yet, before Armstead was released from prison, a letter was sent to various attorneys signed by "Ronald Armstead" stating: "I only testify because I was told by the Hamilton County Prosecutor's office that after my testimony they would see that I go back to the street."

The Ohio Public Defender's office obtained a copy of the letter and sent Thomas W. Kasler, an investigator with the Office of the Nevada Federal Public Defender in Las Vegas, to interview Armstead on May 9, 2000.

Kasler swore, "I showed Ronald Armstead a copy of the document [the letter]... after carefully looking at it for a while, Mr. Armstead said he recognized the letter and it contained his writing. He said he did not remember who he wrote it to."

Prosecutors countered by producing an ex-cop and alleged handwriting expert to say it wasn't Armstead's signature. The courts sided, as in every instance, with the prosecutor's evidence.

Woody Breyer, a prosecutor in the Byrd case, told *Columbus Alive* last year, "You'll never prove there was a deal. There's no proof."

As of press time, eight inmates, black and white, have signed affidavits saying that Armstead fabricated the Byrd confession. The prosecution says the inmates are criminals and shouldn't be believed.

One of the main questions is whether Byrd and Brewer,

young white men, would confess to a black inmate at the racially divided Cincinnati jail.

Robert Pottinger, who was in the van with Byrd, Brewer and Woodall on the day of the murder, confirmed that Byrd and Brewer would not "hang out with them [black people] in jail."

When asked about Armstead, Pottinger said, "Yeah, the nigger... Like we were gonna talk to them," he scoffed. "That's ludicrous. Why would we talk to them in jail? We wouldn't even let them sit with us on the street."

"That was beyond stupid, that they even got that off," Pottinger said of Armstead's testimony. "They probably schooled that man into what to say."

August 30, 2001

13 Days To Die

John W. Byrd Jr. is scheduled to be executed on September 12, 2001, for a crime he insists he did not commit. It may not be unusual to hear protestations of innocence coming from Death Row, but Byrd's case raises so many questions that even some death penalty proponents are concerned about the fallibility of the ultimate, irrevocable punishment: Byrd was convicted based only on flimsy circumstantial evidence and the perjured testimony of a jailhouse snitch. No physical evidence was introduced at trial that links Byrd to the crime for which he was sentenced to die.

Now, prominent politicians from both the Democratic and Republican parties—including death penalty foes like former Governor Jack Gilligan, former U.S. Congressman Tom Luken and conservative State Representative Tom Brinkman—are urging Governor Bob Taft not to execute Byrd.

Byrd is adamant that he did not kill Monte Tewksbury on the night of April 17, 1983. Prosecutors in Hamilton County, where Byrd was convicted, are just as adamant that Byrd is the actual killer. At an August 12, 2001, pro-execution rally in Cincinnati, current Prosecutor Michael Allen called Byrd a "heathen killer" and denounced Gilligan, Luken and Brinkman as "dishonest" for suggesting that Byrd wasn't the murderer.

Included in almost every TV news story on Byrd is the victim's widow, Sharon Tewksbury, usually clutching her late husband's photo and demanding "closure" for her family. Appearing less frequently in the news are Byrd's mother, in a wheelchair, and his sister, pleading for his life.

In Cincinnati and Columbus, death penalty opponents have recently squared off against pro-execution forces, Hamilton County prosecutors and the Tewksbury clan in a series of highly publicized demonstrations. Emotional public arguments about Byrd's impending execution have often obscured the facts, but *Columbus Alive* reporters have spent more than a year sifting through the voluminous public documents generated by the Byrd case. The following is a summation of the investigation.

John Byrd and two friends, John Brewer and William "Danny" Woodall, were arrested at approximately 1 a.m. on April 18, 1983, in a red work truck. The truck matched the description of the vehicle seen fleeing the scene of the King Kwik convenience store where Tewksbury, the store clerk, had been robbed and stabbed.

Items from the King Kwik robbery were found in the truck; the three men were arrested and later charged with robbery and aggravated murder—but only Byrd was charged with stabbing and killing Tewksbury. For Byrd to be eligible for the death penalty under Ohio law, the prosecution had to prove that he purposely killed Tewksbury and that he was the principal offender.

Prosecutors did not seek the death penalty against either Brewer or Woodall, who were convicted of lesser crimes, despite physical evidence linking Brewer to the murder scene. Following their trials, both Brewer and Woodall signed affidavits stating Brewer delivered the death blow to Tewksbury—evidence that courts have refused to consider as grounds for a new evidentiary hearing for Byrd.

Meanwhile, Byrd is preparing to take his final 17 steps from the death house holding cell to be strapped into the electric chair. While he wants to live, Byrd has chosen death by electrocution—Ohio's most brutal form of capital punishment—to protest what he feels is an unjust system that railroaded him onto Death Row.

Ohio Public Defender David Bodiker calls Byrd's trial "a debacle. A disaster." The public defender's office has represented Byrd only after his conviction, and has been cleaning up after what it sees as a shoddy trial defense ever since.

Bodiker points out that Byrd went to trial on August 1, 1983—less than 90 days after his indictment. The rush to court left Byrd virtually defenseless.

"As of July 21, 10 days before trial, the prosecution had not responded to the defendant's request for a bill of particulars, or for basic discovery. The requests for these had been filed in early June. The items were officially provided on July 26, five days before trial... At a pre-trial hearing on July 21, defense counsel complained that they had no information as to why Byrd was the principal offender," Bodiker stressed in an August debate with State Treasurer Joe Deters, the former Hamilton County Prosecutor, at the Columbus Metropolitan Club.

Bodiker emphasized, "There is no evidence that they [Byrd's court-appointed private attorneys] conducted any investigation, that they talked to any witnesses, or that they hired or consulted any experts regarding the blood, the scene of the crime, the weapon used, or how the fatal wound was inflicted on the victim. Before the trial, they informed the prosecution that they had no discovery to provide to them and that they were calling no witnesses."

Court records do not reveal any objections made regarding the hasty nature of the trial. Bodiker says, "The defense counsel in fact seemed eager to accommodate the judge's schedule and to get the trial over with quickly."

Critics of the Hamilton County Prosecutor's office, including the American Civil Liberties Union of Ohio, argue that the aggressive nature of the prosecutor's office, and prosecutors' cozy relationships with common pleas court judges (who all come out of the prosecutor's office), makes Hamilton County defense attorneys the most compliant of Ohio's largest cities.

Deters counters the charge that the trial was unfair, as quoted in a *Cincinnati Post* article: "It's been 18 years and 70 judges—that's seven-zero. Seventy judges have looked at this case and decided he's guilty."

Such hyperbole has been par for the course as the rhetoric on both sides of the Byrd debate has reached a fevered pitch this summer. The ACLU, for instance, easily disputed Deters' exaggerated claim at an August 21 press conference.

"The way they count is, if the Supreme Court declines to hear the case four times, they count that as 36 judges," explained Jeff Gamso, ACLU vice president. "Since John Byrd began his post-conviction proceedings in 1988, he has never been afforded discovery of evidence from the prosecutor's files to prove his claims... All courts have summarily denied Byrd's claims on the basis of 'paper hearings,' without benefit of any actual testimony."

The ACLU press statement noted, "The Ohio Supreme Court has never granted review in over 120 death penalty cases that have been all the way through post-conviction proceedings in this state. The trial and appellate courts in Hamilton County have never granted relief in a single post-conviction case since the inception of Ohio's death penalty in 1981."

Gamso said, "There's never been an evidentiary hearing, it's so misleading to imply fairness. It's always denied."

It's common practice in Hamilton County, and elsewhere, for the post-conviction prosecutor—in this case William Breyer, the brother of Woody Breyer, who prosecuted Byrd at the original trial—to write the trial judge's findings of fact and conclusions of law dismissing defendants' post-conviction petitions. Ostensibly, the judge reviews the prosecutor's findings before issuing them.

In a letter dated March 29, 1991, William Breyer wrote to Judge J. Howard Sundermann of Hamilton County Common Pleas Court, "Since I drafted the proposed entry which resulted in reversal, I must apologize, though I confess that I am still astounded by the interpretation the Court of Appeals reached regarding the language in the entry." The court temporarily reversed Byrd's conviction because Breyer's written record failed to mention that the judge had independently reviewed the prosecutor's findings. Breyer added a new entry to the records stating that the judge had "considered the 'entire record'" in reaching the conclusions written by the prosecutor. The appeals court quickly sided with the prosecutor.

With his August 26, 2001, article "Revisiting the Byrd case," the *Columbus Dispatch*'s Alan Johnson included a chart that listed the five "strongest arguments for Byrd's guilt" from Ohio Attorney General Betty Montgomery's office. That Montgomery's "strongest arguments" are so weak precisely underscores why so many death penalty opponents are rallying behind Byrd—and why even some death penalty supporters question the fairness of Byrd's execution. Court records include ample evidence to refute the state's case for the death penalty.

Montgomery's argument: "Blood drops on Byrd's pants and the van seat—near where Byrd was crouching—were Type O, the same as Tewksbury's. Brewer had no blood on him."

The evidence: The blood in question consisted of two small specks on Byrd's work pants and a blood stain on the side of the driver's seat; it was inconclusive whether the blood was Tewksbury's. Woodall was sitting in the driver's seat where the blood was found and Brewer was in the passenger seat next to him. Woodall had been bleeding that night from a cut above his eye and has the same blood type as Tewksbury.

In an August 17, 1989, motion of summary judgment submitted by William Breyer and then-Hamilton County Prosecuting Attorney Arthur M. Ney Jr., the prosecutors conceded: "The jury was aware that the knife was not identified as the murder weapon, that the blood stains could not be shown to be the victim's, and that the shoe prints were not those of defendant Byrd. These matters simply are not central to the issue of defendant's guilt."

Judge Sundermann's official finding of fact denying Byrd an evidentiary hearing stated, "The source of the blood in the van or on the defendant's pants was not a crucial issue at trial... the blood stains could not be shown to be the victim's."

The state's own admissions about the weakness of the blood evidence has not deterred Montgomery nor the *Cincinnati Post* from championing Byrd's execution based on "blood-stained clothes." Byrd, in previous court proceedings, has asked that the blood evidence and other physical evidence be further tested; prosecutors have fought these motions. In an 1993 affidavit, Woodall claimed that the blood on the van seat resulted from Brewer wiping off the knife blade on the side of the seat after Brewer, not Byrd, stabbed Tewksbury.

Montgomery's argument: "Byrd was wearing Tewksbury's Pulsar watch when arrested."

The evidence: Tewksbury may have been wearing a Pulsar watch when robbed, but the watch was never produced as evidence at trial and its whereabouts, like the murder weapon, are unknown. The *Dispatch* wrote, "Police mistakenly thought it [the Pulsar watch] was Byrd's watch and later gave it to his mother. A police property-room card listing the Pulsar watch was lost; a photocopy showed up the day before Byrd's trial began."

Public defender Dick Vickers told *Columbus Alive*, "There was no watch at trial. It was never introduced into evidence. You have to wonder about the police investigators if they would lose the original evidence log-in card and then mistakenly send evidence in a capital murder case to the mother of the defendant. It's like Keystone Cops."

Byrd's mother acknowledges that the sheriff's department sent her a watch, but it was a Timex, not a Pulsar. Byrd claims he was wearing a Timex watch, not a gold Pulsar.

Montgomery's argument: "At the U-Tote-M convenience store robbery a man identified as Byrd used a knife to attack a door behind which a store clerk was hiding. Dennis Nitz, a customer, testified that Byrd's size and hair color were consistent with the stabber's."

The evidence: After leaving the King Kwik, Woodall later allegedly drove Byrd and Brewer to the U-Tote-M. Byrd was never tried for the U-Tote-M robbery, but investigative records exist.

In a crime lab report dated April 21, 1983, William Dean of the Institute for Forensic Medicine, Toxicology and Criminalistics in Hamilton County, compared the knife, Specimen Q-1, shown in the *Dispatch* and relied on by Montgomery, to the wooden door at the U-Tote-M, Specimen Q-27, and concluded: "The hole in the door, Q-27, was not made by the point of the knife, Q-1."

Also, police found a hair from a single Caucasian in a nylon stocking mask worn during the robbery and concluded: "Comparisons of the hair from Q-8 to hairs from Byrd and Brewer were inconclusive." Dennis Nitz, the witness, told police that the man with the knife was wearing "tan pants"; Byrd's pants were blue.

Gregory W. Meyers, chief counsel of the Public Defender's Death Penalty Division, appealed for Byrd's clemency by stressing that Nitz "unequivocally said that the masked man who had the knife wore tan pants. When arrested a short time later, John Byrd wore blue pants. Tan and blue are too far apart on the color spectrum to create any kind of circumstantial bridge strong enough to prove John Byrd stabbed Monte Tewksbury."

Yet it's precisely that flimsy circumstantial bridge that

the Ohio Supreme Court is relying on to condemn Byrd to death.

Montgomery's argument: "The knife recovered in the truck was identified by Nitz as consistent with the knife he saw in Byrd's hand. Hamilton County Coroner Leonard Parrott said the dimensions of the knife were consistent with Tewksbury's wounds."

The evidence: Prosecutors took a weapon from another crime, the U-Tote-M robbery, that Byrd was never tried for, and theorized that it was the murder weapon in the King Kwik robbery. This is inconsistent with the state's own admissions, since the state concedes "that the knife was not identified as the murder weapon" at Byrd's trial.

The state admitted again it wasn't the murder weapon when the Hamilton County Common Pleas Court wrote in its October 2, 1989, finding of fact: "the knife, could not be shown to be the murder weapon."

Deters and others stress how important the U-Tote-M evidence was in sending Byrd to the electric chair. Deters said, "The [Ohio] Supreme Court itself said the most probative part was the same and similar crime he committed just minutes later in the exact same fashion and Byrd can't deny it."

Montgomery's argument: "Inmate Ronald Armstead testified that Byrd, while in the Hamilton County Jail, bragged to him that he killed Tewksbury. Prison records also indicate Woodall stated Byrd bragged about stabbing Tewksbury."

The evidence: After *Columbus Alive* first reported on jailhouse snitch Ronald Armstead's extensive record of violent felony convictions, the Attorney General and Hamilton County prosecutors have de-emphasized the role of their star witness. State officials are now pushing the physical evidence they earlier conceded was inconclusive, even though they previously argued at trial and at state and federal appeals courts over the years that Armstead's testimony was the sole factor in Byrd's capital conviction and death sentence.

In 1995, Federal Judge James Graham concluded: "The principal evidence presented at trial to suggest that Byrd was the person who stabbed Monte Tewksbury came from Ronald Armstead, who, at the time of trial, was serving a sentence at the Cincinnati workhouse."

Last year, the Sixth Circuit Court of Appeals stated, "All agree that Armstead's testimony was vitally important to the jury's determination that petitioner was the principal offender in the aggravated murder of Monte Tewksbury."

There's a good reason why the state now wants to distance itself from the Byrd trial's most important testimony: It was perjured. Affidavits from eight former workhouse inmates swear that Armstead, a well-known informant and drug addict, manufactured the confession to obtain parole. He was facing up to 15 years in prison for parole violations, and not only failed to disclose that to the jury, but the prosecutor falsely vouched for his truthfulness.

Byrd's supposed bragging to Woodall comes not from Woodall's testimony, but from Armstead's. Prior to his death this year, Woodall, an admitted white supremacist, consistently denied that he ever admitted anything to Ronald Armstead, who is black. In 1993, Woodall signed an affidavit stating that John Brewer was the person who stabbed Monte Tewksbury. In 1989 and 2001, Brewer signed similar affidavits admitting that he, Brewer, murdered Tewksbury.

Byrd, who has consistently denied that he stabbed Tewksbury, has long claimed to *Columbus Alive* and the *Columbus Free Press*, and in a recent WBNS-TV interview, that prosecutors initially approached him about a deal if he testified against Brewer and Woodall. Byrd said he declined since he had no memory of the night. Several witnesses said he had been drinking, smoking pot and taking Quaaludes.

For 15 years, co-defendant John Brewer has admitted that he killed Tewksbury. Robert Pottinger, who was with Byrd, Brewer and Woodall on the day of Tewksbury's slaying and who later served time in the same prison as Woodall on another charge, said, "I talked to Danny Woodall... All the indications I got was it was Johnny Brewer that killed him [Tewksbury]."

Like Byrd, Pottinger says he was offered a deal in exchange for testimony in the Tewksbury case. "They tried to offer me deals, offer me immunity, everything. The man wanted me to say what he wanted me to say," Pottinger told *Columbus Alive*. "When I wouldn't do that, they treated me as a hostile witness."

Pottinger also alleges that before his testimony at Byrd's and Brewer's trials, he was coached by a prosecutor in the prosecutor's office. He recalled, "[During a trial], I said, 'Hey man, he just told me the answers to the questions up there in his office that he's asking me right now.' Everybody ignored it. I said that in the courtroom, on the stand."

Ohio's battle over the life and death of John Byrd is also a question about whether our government makes mistakes. Since 1973, 92 wrongly convicted Death Row inmates have been released from other government jurisdictions. And there have been plenty of mistakes made in the Byrd case. The prosecutors admit they couldn't produce the murder weapon, the watch, or any other physical evidence linking Byrd to the actual killing of Tewksbury. They never did a DNA test on the blood on Byrd's pants.

Despite misleading news accounts suggesting Governor Bob Taft's choice is either to kill Byrd or set him free, the public defenders representing Byrd have never asked for his release. At Byrd's August 20, 2001, clemency hearing, Greg W. Meyers told the Ohio Parole Board, "[Byrd] will never walk the street, nor should he," but that the circumstances surrounding Byrd's death sentence "ought to leave you feeling queasy about whether we should kill John Byrd."

Ironically, one person who appears to agree with Meyers' call for life in prison without parole is Monte Tewksbury's widow, Sharon, who told the *Columbus Dispatch* that neither she nor her husband were "strong supporters of the death penalty."

The *Dispatch* quoted Mrs. Tewksbury as saying, "I would be fine with prison for life without parole. But I can't feel confident he would be in prison for life."

The final decision is up to Governor Taft, who has the power to commute Byrd's death sentence to life in prison without parole. Howard Tolley Jr., a human rights expert and professor of political science at the University of Cincinnati, told *Alive*, "Ohio must not dehumanize the condemned. John Byrd is a dangerous criminal who should suffer the retribution of a life term. His execution would be a gross miscarriage of justice—the trial was egregiously tainted by perjured testimony and there are substantial doubts that the actual killer was sentenced to death."

August 30, 2001

"Byrd Never Left The Van"

John W. Byrd Jr. was not the knife-wielding man in a robbery committed later the same night Monte Tewksbury was murdered, according to a sworn statement signed last week by Robert E. Pottinger Jr. Pottinger claims he was with Byrd and two others at the second robbery the night of April 17, 1983.

The Ohio Supreme Court ruled that Byrd's identification as the knife wielder in the U-Tote-M convenience store robbery was "highly probative" evidence that he stabbed Tewksbury to death at a King Kwik store, a crime for which Byrd is scheduled to be executed September 12.

But in an August 31, 2001, affidavit obtained by *Columbus Alive*, Pottinger—who says he was picked up by Byrd, John Brewer and William Woodall after Tewksbury's murder—states that Byrd "was heavily intoxicated that night, had passed out and did not participate in the U-Tote-M robbery."

"The witnesses who identified Byrd as the masked man who stabbed at the door of the restroom in which the store's clerk had hidden were wrong," Pottinger's affidavit states. "Byrd never left the van during this robbery."

Pottinger's affidavit conforms with two statements

signed by Brewer in which Brewer says that he, not Byrd, killed Tewksbury. In a 1989 affidavit, Brewer says that when he and Byrd entered the King Kwik store, Byrd "staggered...and was having a hard time standing up." In an affidavit signed this year, Brewer says Byrd "appeared to be highly intoxicated" the night of the murder.

In 1993, Woodall also signed an affidavit swearing Brewer was the killer. "John Byrd Jr. appeared highly intoxicated and was almost unable to walk," Woodall stated. "When John E. Brewer exited the King Kwik store and entered the vehicle in which we were riding, the knife he was carrying was covered with blood... Brewer attempted to wipe the knife blade on the right-hand side of the driver's seat in the vehicle."

Both Byrd's co-defendants, and now Pottinger, say Brewer stabbed Tewksbury. "I talked to Danny Woodall. I was in the same prison with him for awhile... All the indications I got was it was Johnny Brewer that killed him," Pottinger told *Alive*.

At both the King Kwik and U-Tote-M robberies, Brewer's footprint was found on the store counters.

Pottinger, whose possible involvement in one or both of the robberies was revealed in the August 30, 2001, issue of *Columbus Alive*, does not say in his affidavit who entered the King Kwik with Brewer.

But Kim Hamer, Byrd's sister, says Pottinger admitted to her in a telephone conversation on August 29 that he was the man who stabbed at the restroom door in an attempt to get at the U-Tote-M store clerk who had hidden inside.

Jim Henneberry, a U-Tote-M employee, described the man with the knife as wearing "tan pants" and a "jacket" that was "red and black." A U-Tote-M customer, Dennis Nitz, also told police that the man with the knife was wearing "tan pants." The witnesses described both U-Tote-M robbers as wearing masks.

When Byrd, Brewer and Woodall were arrested shortly after the second robbery, Byrd was wearing blue slacks and a sweater with wide blue, yellow and black stripes. Brewer and Woodall were wearing blue jeans.

Prosecutor Woody Breyer conceded to the jury that, despite the eyewitness identification of a knife wielder in a black and red jacket and tan pants, that Byrd was wearing the "same sweater he was wearing when he left Northside, [the] striped sweater."

In order to explain away two eyewitness accounts of a robber with "tan pants," prosecutor Breyer offered the jury his own theory that Nitz must have been wearing the tan pants: "You have seen them all that they were all blue. I speculate that that tan he wore he [Nitz] had tan pants. I will tell you this, Nitz wasn't concerned with what color pants he had on, and he is trying to help the police. He made a mistake. He's a kid, lucky to be alive today, given that one fault, that faulty recall."

The prosecutors' forensic reports determined that a knife found in the red work van when Byrd, Brewer and Woodall were arrested was not, in fact, the knife wielded at the U-Tote-M scene. Pottinger was not in the van when the three were arrested.

Pottinger previously told *Alive* that, following the arrest of the three co-defendants, he was detained in a juvenile facility on pending murder charges but ultimately was never charged with anything. A major reason why, Pottinger says in his affidavit, is that "Byrd, Brewer and

Woodall later told me that they had agreed to keep my name out of the case because I was only 17."

Pottinger was convicted in 1987 of receiving stolen property and was placed on parole. He was convicted of robbery in 1989 and spent nearly 11 years in prison. He is now on parole in Tennessee.

With Pottinger's affidavit discrediting the claim that Byrd was the man with the knife in both robberies the night of April 17, 1983, the only remaining evidence that Byrd killed Tewksbury is the testimony of Ronald Armstead, who claimed that Byrd confessed to the crime while both were in the Hamilton County Jail.

Armstead had been arrested 22 times before his testimony at Byrd's trial. He has been arrested at least four times since, most recently in 1996.

A concerted effort by *Columbus Alive* to locate Armstead for comment has determined that he is working on an Alaskan cruise ship. Members of Armstead's own family said they were unable to get word to him that one of his sisters died on August 10.

Judging from the comments of a rental agent at the Las Vegas apartment complex at which Armstead lived until recently, Armstead is apparently a good liar. The agent told Thomas W. Casler, an investigator with the Office of the Nevada Federal Public Defender, that she decided not to sue Armstead for the five weeks' rent he owed when he left because he claimed he had just been diagnosed with cancer. The rental agent said she later learned from a family member that this was not true.

Co-written with Martin Yant
September 6, 2001

The Fifth Man
In The Van

He had a large knife, with which he had stabbed someone before. It was his idea to rob the King Kwik store in suburban Cincinnati, during which clerk Monte Tewksbury was fatally stabbed. He later bragged that he was the killer.

His name was John Brewer, not John Byrd Jr., whose execution for killing Tewksbury was postponed by a federal appeals court on Monday, the same day Governor Bob Taft denied Byrd clemency. Brewer has admitted to the slaying in two affidavits, but the courts that have considered appeals so far didn't find Brewer's confessions credible.

John Lee Fryman does. Unlike the judges, Fryman says, he was with Brewer, Byrd and their co-defendant, William Woodall, as they planned the King Kwik robbery on April 17, 1983. In fact, Brewer tried to get Fryman to go along. He declined, Fryman says, because he had plans for another robbery that night.

Fryman, who is serving a life sentence for murder at Warren Correctional Institution, says prosecutors will point to his record and attack his credibility the same way they have desperately tried to discredit Robert E. Pottinger Jr.'s claim in last week's *Columbus Alive* that he was with Brewer, Byrd and Woodall during the robbery at U-Tote-M convenience store about an hour after the robbery in which Tewksbury was killed.

Pottinger told *Alive* that Byrd was so drunk at that time he had passed out and did not leave their van at the U-Tote-M.

Fryman said he spent the morning and early afternoon of April 17, 1983, driving around the Northside area of Cincinnati with Brewer, Byrd and another man. Fryman said the four of them drove around "drinking, getting high and other good stuff" until early in the afternoon. "It doesn't surprise me that [Pottinger says] Bird Dog [Byrd] was passed out, because he had had a fifth of Daniels before noon," Fryman said.

"I was up front with John Brewer, who was begging me to be the driver for them that night," Fryman said. "We went and he showed me the place they were going to rob."

Fryman said he turned down Brewer and eventually dropped them off at Brewer's house. "Brewer talked Woodall into being the driver later that day," Fryman said. "The only reason Woodall was involved is because I turned them down."

Fryman said it was clear that Brewer was the mastermind of the robberies. "He was the one giving the orders. He was the one who cased the place. He was the one who tried to get me to be the driver," Fryman said. "He turned the radio up as I was driving so the two in the back couldn't hear what he was telling me," Fryman said. "He acted like the guys in the back were flunkies."

Brewer was definitely not a flunky. Fryman said Brewer once had stabbed someone during a fight with the same eight- or nine-inch knife Brewer had with him the day Tewksbury was stabbed to death. In addition, Fryman said, Brewer bragged to him and many others when they were in prison together in Lucasville that he, not Byrd, had killed Tewksbury.

Fryman said that when he heard about the arrest of Brewer, Byrd and Woodall on the radio the next day, he went to Pottinger's house, packed him up and drove Pottinger to Florida because he had heard that police were looking for a fourth suspect.

When Pottinger was told about Fyrman's comments, he said: "He's telling the truth."

Columbus Alive broke the story concerning Pottinger's role in the U-Tote-M robbery on August 30, 2001, in an article titled "The man in the plaid shirt?" The story documented evidence in police files linking Pottinger to both the King Kwik robbery, where Tewksbury was killed, and the U-Tote-M robbery. Pottinger, then 17 years old, confirmed to *Alive* in an interview that he had been jailed as a "murder suspect" in the Training Institute of Central Ohio, a juvenile facility.

The next day, at the request of *Columbus Alive*, Pottinger signed an affidavit notarized in Tennessee. On Tuesday, September 4, John Byrd's sister, Kim Hamer, turned over a copy of the affidavit to Governor Taft's office along with a tape of a conversation she had recorded with Pottinger.

On Thursday, September 6, *Alive* published a story on Pottinger's affidavit and the new evidence establishing him as a fourth man and murder suspect in the Tewksbury case. As *Alive* hit the streets, two members of the Ohio Attorney General's office and a law enforcement officer flew to Tennessee for what appeared to be an old-fashioned rousting and interrogation of Pottinger. The attorney general's office confirmed the trip to the *Columbus Dispatch*.

"I just got released from the TBI [Tennessee Bureau of Investigation] about five minutes ago," Pottinger told *Alive*. "There were some people from the [Ohio] Attorney General's office up there... They come and got me from work this morning."

The focus of the attorney general's questioning concerned the affidavit. Pottinger said, "I told them it's valid."

Pottinger recounted his interrogation and exchange with an unidentified man from Ohio: "The man was standing there telling me, you know, that paper you signed doesn't mean shit," and Pottinger replied, "Yeah, you flew down here from Cincinnati, or from Columbus, to tell me that, didn't ya... He couldn't say nothing."

"They asked me about the U-Tote-M. They asked me if Johnny was passed out, and I told them exactly this: Johnny Byrd was not in the U-Tote-M store... I was very clear.

"That's the exact words: 'Johnny Byrd was never in the U-Tote-M store, never,'" Pottinger explained. "They asked me how I knew and I told them I was in the van... and they was arrested a couple hours later. And I told them they let me out of the van.

"Dude, I'm positive, 100 percent without a doubt, John William Byrd Jr. was not in the U-Tote-M... I'm standing by the affidavit and, whatever happens, you know, I guess it's time for me to pay the piper, huh?" Pottinger said, "I'm not going to fight them or nothing. I'm not going to argue with 'em. I'm gonna go. I even gave the guy my phone number, you know, my pager number. Page me, and I'll turn myself in."

When Brewer signed two affidavits stating that he did

the stabbing at the King Kwik, the attorney general's office and Hamilton County prosecutors claimed Brewer had nothing to lose, despite the parole implications. Brewer is serving a life sentence for his role in the King Kwik robbery.

But the state has had a harder time explaining Pottinger's affidavit, which Hamilton County Prosecutor Michael Allen dismissed as "nonsense."

When asked why he was coming forward now, Pottinger said, "I think I'm doing everything I can do to help me clear my conscience… Of course I'm afraid. Of course I am, man, you know? I'm afraid I'm facing some years in prison again. I've gotten out, I've worked, I've not been in any trouble, I go to see my parole officer regularly… I have a nice girlfriend, I've had a job."

"Dude, I take my girlfriend's little boy to karate practice and stuff man, I take him to school and pick him up in the afternoons," Pottinger continued. "Do you know how much I'm losing? I'm losing my whole life by putting this out there. I had to. I mean, I wouldn't even be a man if I didn't."

Co-written with Martin Yant
September 13, 2001

New Evidence
Backs Statements

Mounting evidence backs a man's claim that he was with John Brewer and John W. Byrd Jr. the day Byrd later allegedly killed a suburban Cincinnati convenience store clerk. A new witness also supports the contention—made since he was first arrested 18 years ago—that Byrd was too drunk to do much of anything the night Monte Tewksbury was murdered.

Because of Byrd's condition, John Lee Fryman told *Columbus Alive* last week, he believed Robert E. Pottinger Jr.'s claim in the previous issue of *Alive* that Byrd had passed out and did not participate in a robbery after Tewksbury's murder on April 17, 1983.

Byrd's execution for the Tewksbury murder was scheduled for September 12, 2001, but on September 10 was stayed until October 8 by a federal appeals court.

But that didn't stop Ohio Attorney General Betty Montgomery from pursuing Byrd's immediate execution.

Just after the worst attack on the United States in history, during which the Supreme Court justices were holed up in a bunker, Montgomery filed an unsuccessful motion on September 11, 2001, asking the high court to overturn the stay before Byrd's death warrant expired at midnight

Wednesday. "We were quite surprised, considering the circumstances," an employee at the Supreme Court clerk's office said.

The state of Texas, with its reputation for zealously carrying out executions, appeared enlightened by comparison. Governor Rick Perry stayed an execution planned for September 11 for 30 days to ensure the condemned inmate had "full and complete access to the court system," which the Supreme Court's closure precluded.

Because of threats Pottinger says were made against him by Montgomery's office after his statement became known, the Tennessee resident was reluctant to talk about Fryman's comments last week other than to say Fryman was "telling the truth."

Pottinger elaborated this week, though, including commenting on Fryman's claim that he took Pottinger to Florida the day after Tewksbury's murder when he learned that police believed a fourth man was with Byrd, Brewer and driver William Woodall during one or both robberies.

"I did go to Florida with Fryman," Pottinger said.

Pottinger also said Fryman had a friend with them when they rode around the Cincinnati area earlier the day of the robberies and murder.

Fryman, who is serving a life sentence for murder at Warren Correctional Institution, identified the man who was with him as Tim Taylor. Taylor confirmed that he had on occasion been with Fryman when Fryman picked up some Northside friends. Taylor said it would be hard to say for sure if one of those days was April 17, 1983, however. When he was told that Fryman said they stole some gas grills together that night, Taylor said that "definitely was a possibility."

Taylor added that he stopped running around with Fryman shortly after that because of Fryman's tendency to get into trouble.

Pottinger also backed Fryman's claim that Brewer had stabbed someone in a fight shortly before the stabbing of Tewksbury.

"Yeah, I heard that Brewer had stabbed somebody," Pottinger said. "There was some blood on the front of Fryman's little silver car. That was the story. It was a silver Pinto station wagon. We used to drive around in it."

Pottinger mentioned being with Fryman when he testified at Byrd's trial in the following exchange:

Question: And where did you meet him [Byrd]?
Answer: My house.
Q: What time?
A: 12 o'clock.
Q: Did you do any beer-drinking or...?
A: Yes, sir.
Q: What else?
A: Smoked a little bit of pot.
Q: Did you find John Brewer?
A: Yes, sir.
Q: Where?
A: Working with his father.
Q: Did you call him off the job?
A: Yes, sir.
Q: And then what happened?
A: We went riding around.
Q: In whose car?
A: Johnny Fryman's.
Q: Who?

A: Johnny Fryman's.

Q: Where did you ride?

A: Just around Northside.

Q: Did you eventually get in touch with Woodall?

A: Yes, sir.

Q: When, when did you have all three of them together. That is Byrd, Brewer and Woodall?

A: Around 6:30 to 7 that evening.

In a letter to *Columbus Alive* in response to *Alive*'s revelation that Pottinger was present for the second robbery, John Byrd wrote: "It's just unreal. What else is hidden away, or has been destroyed by Hamilton County prosecutors? The prosecutors are always talking about something being withheld. This new information that came out about Mr. Pottinger had to be withheld from my trial counsel... If they would have had that kind of information, there's no doubt when Mr. Pottinger was put on the stand they would have used it.

"The constant lying from both the Hamilton County prosecutors and the attorney general's office is beyond comprehension. The lies don't match up [to] the facts. But yet I'm called a liar and a number of other names."

Meanwhile, Ohio Public Defender David Bodiker confirmed the existence of two affidavits Woodall signed in 1989, in addition to one signed in 1993, in which Woodall stated that Brewer, not Byrd, killed Tewksbury. Bodiker said his office also had a copy of a letter in which inmate Tom Sergeant offered to give the Hamilton County prosecutors the name of the juvenile involved in the robbery, in an apparent reference to Pottinger.

Alive obtained an Ohio Department of Rehabilitation

and Corrections document showing that Hamilton County prosecutors and State Trooper Howard Hudson questioned Woodall on January 29, 2001, just before Woodall was taken to the hospital with "Chest Pains, Possible Heart Attack" at 3:35 p.m.

Although Woodall refused to sign an affidavit saying Byrd killed Tewksbury, and had signed three affidavits saying Brewer did it—Brewer himself admitted to the killing in two affidavits—the prosecutors and Hudson signed statements claiming that the terminally ill Woodall told them Byrd did it.

According to their accounts at Byrd's clemency hearing, the prosecutors returned two days later to talk to Woodall at the OSU Medical Center while Woodall was writing his will. Once again, they failed to secure an affidavit, a taped statement or any other definitive evidence. Yet conservative Sixth Circuit Judge Alice M. Batchelder insisted on referring to the prosecution's statements as a deathbed confession by Woodall in her dissent of the court's action to stay Brewer's execution.

Woodall's medical records show that, although Woodall had terminal cancer, the prison was treating him with low-level painkillers that were the equivalent of aspirin. Prison sources claim that the state was doing everything possible to pressure Woodall into signing an affidavit implicating Byrd for the murder of Tewksbury.

And even more troubling facts are being unearthed as Byrd's attorneys prepare their final defense:

• The Ohio Public Defender's Memorandum in Support of Jurisdiction filed with the Ohio Supreme Court on August 22 notes, "The police in their radio broadcast [the night of the murder] made it clear that they were searching for an individual who was wearing plaid. In fact, the police originally stopped another vehicle in the immediate area of King Kwik at least partially based on the fact that one of the occupants of the vehicle was wearing plaid."

Fryman, who was with Byrd and Brewer earlier the day of their arrest, said that Brewer definitely was wearing a shirt at the time. Fryman said he believed the shirt was plaid, but he couldn't say for sure. When Brewer was arrested, he was only wearing a thin mesh T-shirt.

• Informants like Ronald Armstead, who testified that Byrd confessed to him that he killed Tewksbury, are plentiful in Hamilton County death penalty cases. Jailhouse snitches have testified for the prosecutors in no fewer than 10 capital trials in Hamilton County.

"The only...jailhouse snitches to testify in capital cases, to my knowledge, all come from Hamilton County," said Bodiker. "You have to wonder why their criminals are so civic-minded, or why the prosecutors are so lucky in only that county."

• Dennis Nitz, one of two witnesses at the second robbery, told *Columbus Alive* that he stands by his testimony that the robber wielding a knife wore tan pants. Byrd, the alleged knife wielder, was wearing blue pants that night. In his closing argument, the Hamilton County prosecutor who handled the case said Nitz was mistaken about the pants' color.

Co-written with Martin Yant
September 20, 2001

Finally, A Real Appeal

In a stunning decision on October 9, 2001, the Sixth Circuit U.S. Court of Appeals stayed the execution of Death Row inmate John W. Byrd Jr. for at least 45 days while a federal district court investigates Byrd's claim that he is innocent of the stabbing for which he was sentenced to die.

Meanwhile, new information obtained by *Columbus Alive* points to a troubling aspect of Byrd's original prosecution: that Debbie Brewer, the sister of Byrd's accomplice John Brewer, may have been a police informant who led investigators away from her brother and toward Byrd as the suspected killer of Monte Tewksbury.

What the Sixth Circuit Court wants investigated is the role jailhouse snitches played in Byrd's conviction; whether there was a deal between jailhouse snitch Ronald Armstead and the Hamilton County Prosecutor's office; and whether there was any collusion between the prosecutor's office, the Ohio Attorney General's office and the Ohio Department of Corrections regarding the Byrd case.

A majority of the judges ordered that the chief judge of the Southern District of Ohio appoint a magistrate judge "to promptly conduct an appropriate factual hearing." The circuit court directed, "The hearing should develop a record with regard to John Byrd's claim of innocence presented to the Ohio courts but on which no testimony of witnesses or evidence was taken."

Despite the Hamilton County Prosecutor's disingenuous mantra that "70 judges have looked at this case and decided he's guilty," this will be the first evidentiary hearing in the Byrd case since the original 1983 trial.

The circuit court specifically stated: "We direct that the scope of the factual inquiry conducted by the Magistrate Judge shall include testimony relating to matters set forth in the affidavits of John Brewer, Dan Cahill, Darryl Messer, Roger Hall and Benny Fields." The latter four men served in prison with Brewer over the years and all signed affidavits stating that Brewer admitted to or made incriminating statements related to the killing.

Brewer, co-defendant with Byrd, signed affidavits both in 1989 and earlier this year admitting that he, not Byrd, was the killer of Cincinnati convenience store clerk Tewksbury. Brewer is currently serving a life term for his role in the Tewksbury murder.

Brewer's footprint was found on the counter at the King Kwik convenience store where Tewksbury was slain. The Ohio Public Defender's office contends that the decision to indict and try Byrd for capital murder never made sense, since the prosecution conceded there was no physical evidence directly linking Byrd to the murder.

Sources close to the investigation claim that one reason Byrd, instead of Brewer, was originally indicted for capital murder rests with Brewer's sister Debbie. Sources say she became a police informant following her arrest in a drug bust at the time and was helping develop evidence in the Tewksbury case.

Initially Debbie Brewer's evidence pointed to Robert

Pottinger. The prosecutor's office instead focused on either Byrd or Brewer as the murder suspect. Byrd's attorneys point out that it would have been difficult for the prosecutor to get a capital conviction against Pottinger, a juvenile at the time, and that this may have influenced the failure to investigate him fully as a suspect.

John Lee Fryman—who, court records indicate, was with Byrd and Brewer earlier in the day on which Tewksbury was killed—says he believes Brewer committed the murder.

Fryman, now an inmate at Warren Correctional Institute, told *Columbus Alive* that Debbie Brewer became a snitch after being busted for drugs. Debbie originally "set up" Fryman and Pottinger as suspects in the Tewksbury robbery and murder, Fryman claims. He says she encouraged them to stay at her apartment and "smoke one more joint" until the police arrived to arrest them. Fryman says that when it turned out that John Brewer was a chief suspect, his sister then put the word out that it was John Byrd who killed Tewksbury.

At the secret grand jury proceedings where Byrd was indicted for capital murder with death penalty specifications, the prosecutor relied on the testimony of Leroy Tunstall, the owner of the truck that was used in the crime. Tunstall's employee, William "Danny" Woodall (the third convicted accomplice), drove Brewer and Byrd to the King Kwik. In a document released by the prosecution, Tunstall told the grand jury that he overheard Debbie Brewer talking to her brother on the phone, crying and screaming, "Johnny Byrd did it."

If Debbie Brewer had been called to testify at trial, it may have come out, according to the sources, that she was a police informant. When asked about the possibility that Debbie Brewer was a police informant, Ohio Public Defender David Bodiker said, "I think she was a snitch. I think she bought her brother John better treatment."

Instead of Debbie, at trial the prosecutors used a jailhouse snitch—the former heroin addict, pimp and violent felon Ronald Armstead—to provide the only "direct evidence" against Byrd.

The Sixth Circuit Court has ordered that the magistrate examine "Documents prepared by the Hamilton County Prosecutor's office and/or Hamilton County Sheriff's Department authorizing, directing or identifying Ronald Armstead, Virgil Jordan, Marvin Randolph and Robert Jones to be questioned in matters relating to the issue of innocence." *Columbus Alive* first raised the issue of the credibility of Armstead's story in the August 3, 2000, article "Convicted by a snitch."

Armstead was released from prison a few months after his testimony at the Byrd trial and later acknowledged to a federal public defender investigator that he wrote a letter reminding the Hamilton County Prosecutor of their "deal." An extensive investigation by *Alive* has turned up evidence that Armstead was arrested for robberies in Las Vegas in the 1990s and that he is now apparently spending most of his time offshore working on a cruise ship. When asked whether the difficulty of locating Armstead would be a problem for Byrd's defense, Bodiker replied that it's "the prosecutor's problem."

"Mr. Armstead has made several substantially inconsistent statements regarding John Byrd. In one statement he says that he went to prosecutors following remarks that Byrd made on May 26 when he and John were watching

TV, but we know that he testified before the grand jury a few weeks earlier," Bodiker said.

"Armstead provided inaccurate testimony; he swore that he had nothing over his head, which was a lie; he fudged on other statements, particularly his criminal record," Bodiker charged. "I think the only thing he got right was his mother's name."

According to documents filed by the Ohio Public Defender's office, Hamilton County prosecutors have used snitches in at least 10 Death Row convictions. The public defender could find no similar use of snitches in any other Ohio county.

The Sixth Circuit Court also specifically ordered, "Documents prepared or received by the Hamilton County Prosecutor's office or Hamilton County Sheriff's Department or Cincinnati Police Department relating to Ronald Armstead's incarceration, testimony and parole revocation hearing and disposition" are to be examined.

Also, the circuit court order mandates that "Documents or reports received by the Attorney General's office or Hamilton County Prosecutor's office from the Ohio Department of Corrections or its institutions relating to this matter" must be examined.

Critics of the Hamilton County Prosecutor's office charge that the Attorney General's office and the Department of Corrections have worked closely in covering up evidence in the Byrd case. *Columbus Alive* acquired records indicating that prison officials were treating Woodall, who was serving a life sentence for the Tewksbury murder and died earlier this year, with the equivalent of over-the-counter painkillers for his cancer. Prison sources claim that Woodall was being pressured to sign an affidavit saying Byrd was the killer, which Woodall refused to do, and after questioning from the prosecutor's office and a state trooper, Woodall went to the hospital with heart attack symptoms. Woodall previously had signed three affidavits saying that Brewer was the actual killer.

Co-written with Martin Yant
October 18, 2001

Sideshow Justice

What do you do if you're the prosecution in the John Byrd evidentiary hearing and defense witness after witness corroborates Byrd's claim of actual innocence in the murder of Monte Tewksbury? When you don't have any physical evidence against Byrd and your "star" witness is a violent ex-felon and notorious jailhouse snitch whose whereabouts are conveniently unknown?

What do you do? You attack the Ohio Public Defender's office.

What started off promisingly for Byrd on Monday ended on Friday with Ohio Public Defender David Bodiker stepping down from Byrd's defense team while Byrd's lawyers were threatened with disciplinary action and possible criminal indictments.

Arrogant prosecution witnesses waiting to testify were right when they repeatedly complained about Byrd's hearing being "a joke," but for the wrong reason. It wasn't Byrd's evidence that was the problem. It was the prosecution's lack of evidence that caused them to attack the public defender's office. The federal appeals court that ordered the hearing needs to look into U.S. Magistrate Michael Merz's decisions that allowed prosecutors to put public defenders on the stand in a sideshow that distracted from the purpose of the trial: Byrd's claims of innocence.

John Brewer kicked off the circus on Monday, November 5, 2001, with detailed testimony about how *he* stabbed Tewksbury instead of the man who is facing death for the crime. Brewer's footprint was on the counter of the convenience store where Tewksbury was murdered and his pockets reflected the contents of the cash register. Brewer, serving more than 41 years in prison for his participation in the murder, admitted over and over again to being the actual killer.

It's understandable that after James Canepa, the assistant attorney general, repeatedly and repetitively grilled Brewer, the exasperated convict asked the rhetorical question, "Are you retarded?" But hey, this is Ohio, where intentionally sounding mentally deficient is often a prerequisite for holding public office.

Later witnesses Benny Fields, Darryl Messer and Roger Hall testified that Brewer told them years ago that he, not Byrd, killed Tewksbury.

Two black inmates, Elwood Jones and Abdul Mughni, testified that Ronald Armstead, the jailhouse snitch in the case, had laughed and bragged about cutting a deal with Hamilton County prosecutors to escape the remainder of a 15-year prison sentence in exchange for his testimony against Byrd. Inmate Oliver Duff III swore he overheard Armstead and another inmate saying "they were going to work the case for the prosecutor… in order to get leverage in their own personal cases."

Prosecution documents concede that prosecutors had no direct evidence against Byrd other than the preposterous testimony of Armstead, the "star" witness. Armstead, who is black, claimed that Byrd, an admitted white racist at the time, confessed to him while in jail. Denver Nicely Jr., Byrd's former jailmate, told the court that Byrd was "extremely" racist and "never associated with black people" while in the Hamilton County Jail.

The prosecution also relied on circumstantial evidence, without any direct evidence, that Byrd wielded a knife at a second robbery the night of the Tewksbury murder. Then on Tuesday, Robert Pottinger told the court that Byrd was passed out in the van during that robbery and that it was he—not Byrd—who went into the store with Brewer, thus destroying the "highly probative evidence" that the Ohio Supreme Court relied on to sanction Byrd's execution.

Lost in all the shouting was the potential testimony of John Lee Fryman. Fryman says he was ready to reiterate his claim—first made in the September 13 issue of *Columbus Alive*—that, when he was with Byrd and Brewer before the robberies, Brewer had a large knife like the one used to kill Tewksbury and Byrd was stone drunk. Fryman was subpoenaed but never called to the stand to testify.

Martin Yant, co-author of this column, was subpoenaed by the attorney general to testify about the Pottinger affidavit obtained by *Columbus Alive*. Yant was also never called to the stand.

Among the other subpoenaed witnesses who didn't take the stand was Dan Cahill, who swore in an affidavit earlier this year that he served time in prisons where Brewer, Byrd and accomplice Danny Woodall were inmates, and that all three confirmed it was Brewer, not Byrd, who killed Tewksbury.

Despite the staggering amount of evidence in Byrd's favor, the prosecutors were successful in spinning their version of the trial to most news outlets in Ohio.

Wes Hills of the *Dayton Daily News* dutifully reported, "As with Monday's testimony, the parade of murderers, robbers, muggers and arsonists continued earlier Tuesday." Funny, Hills failed to mention that the word of oft-convicted felon Armstead, in jail at the time for assaulting a nurse and a prison guard with a hospital bed crank, was good enough for the Hamilton County prosecutors when Byrd was sent to Death Row.

Another "joke" was the misleading coverage of the hearing by Associated Press correspondent James Hannah. Instead of sticking to the facts, which the AP generally prides itself in doing, Hannah reported on November 8 that Byrd "suffered a setback... when a prosecutor testified that attorneys who represented Byrd in his 1983 murder trial told him that Byrd had admitted stabbing the victim."

Most Ohio news outlets, which relied on AP's coverage of the hearing, made Byrd's "setback" their headline without realizing that Hannah neglected to report that the prosecutor who made that claim, Daniel Breyer, happened to be the one who originally prosecuted Byrd, and that his brother, William Breyer, handled Hamilton County's state appeals. How hearsay evidence—which Byrd's trial attorney disputed—from such a prejudiced witness could be considered a "setback" is hard to fathom.

With little else going for it other than the *Dayton Daily News* and AP reporters, the prosecution proceeded to hammer the public defender's office for not turning over all the affidavits signed by John Brewer containing his confession to the murder. Only reporter Alan Johnson of the *Columbus Dispatch* seemed willing to point out that one of the affidavits was a duplicate and that Brewer admitted the same thing in all of them—that he, not Byrd, killed Tewksbury.

Lost again in the reporting were *Columbus Alive*'s well-documented facts that the prosecutor had not only failed to turn over evidence regarding Pottinger as a murder suspect in Byrd's original trial, but that Daniel Breyer vouched for Armstead's false testimony that he wasn't facing any additional time in prison at the time of Byrd's original trial.

Whatever happens in the ongoing freak show orchestrated by Magistrate Merz and the prosecutors, the public in Ohio should demand that Byrd receive a fair trial—something he's been denied from the beginning by prosecutors with political ambitions who will say and do anything to win. Unlike sporting contests, winning at any cost equals death in this deadly and unprincipled game.

Co-written with Martin Yant
November 15, 2001

Infallible In Ohio

After spending more than 18 years on Death Row, John W. Byrd Jr.'s fate may finally be decided this week. U.S. Magistrate Michael Merz's fact-finding report to the Sixth Circuit U.S. Court of Appeals in Cincinnati—following an unprecedented evidentiary hearing on Byrd's claim of innocence in the stabbing of convenience store clerk Monte Tewksbury—is due on November 30, 2001.

The more Merz sticks to the actual testimony of witnesses, and avoids the sideshow orchestrated by the Ohio Attorney General's office and Hamilton County prosecutors, the better off Byrd will be. Essentially, the AG's office showed up with no case—no physical evidence and without their notorious snitch, Ronald Armstead. But Merz let prosecutors create a case by allowing them to question Byrd's post-conviction public defenders and turn the hearing into an inquisition over duplicate and redundant affidavits, rather than sticking with the assignment of hearing Byrd's claims of actual innocence.

The AG's office, through legal sleight-of-hand, appeared to be pulling a rabbit out of its prosecutorial hat while hiding facts favoring Byrd's innocence up its sleeve. Death penalty watchdogs have long charged that the snitch-happy Hamilton County prosecutors are out of control. With the attorney general's attack on the Ohio Public Defender's office at the mid-November hearing, the ethics of the state's highest law enforcement officer must also be called into question.

Sure, the PD's office is staffed by anti-death penalty zealots—that's their job. Just like the AG's office is staffed by spin doctors and attorneys who will swear under oath that Betty Montgomery is even more infallible than the Pope. In their black-and-white world, prosecutors never make mistakes.

But five days prior to Byrd's hearing, the Ninth Circuit U.S. Court of Appeals overturned the death sentence of a San Bernardino, California, man who was convicted of a double murder in 1983—the same year as Byrd's original conviction. All 11 judges agreed that the court-appointed lawyer did a horrendous job and failed to adequately represent Demetrie L. Mayfield. Recall that at Byrd's original trial, his court-appointed attorney basically failed to mount a defense—despite the existence in police files of a fourth suspect, Robert Pottinger, who turned up in a recent *Columbus Alive* investigation. The similarity between the Byrd case and the overturned California case is striking.

And just two weeks prior to Byrd's evidentiary hearing, a federal court in Chicago awarded James Newsome $15 million for being wrongly imprisoned for 15 years in the slaying of a grocery store owner. The jury determined that Newsome had been framed by two Chicago homicide detectives who coached eyewitnesses. The Byrd case is rife with the same allegations, but in his case the witnesses were snitches, and the key eyewitness, John Brewer, now admits that he did the stabbing. Plus, Brewer's footprint was on the convenience store counter and the apparent contents of the cash register were in his possession.

During Byrd's week-long hearing, a Virginia circuit court judge overturned the murder conviction of Jeffrey David Cox after he spent 11 years in prison. Unlike Ohio, Virginia's Attorney General supported the action. Montgomery the omniscient, rather than acknowledge the occasional wrongdoing in the real world, would instead err on the side of killing the innocent—no doubt a practice favored by the Taliban and other rogue states along with Ohio.

The same day Cox was freed, four men were freed of murder charges in Illinois when DNA testing exonerated them. The Hamilton County prosecutor's office vigorously opposed additional blood testing requested by the public defender's office in the Byrd case, arguing that it didn't matter since Armstead, their jailhouse snitch (and violent felon), was such a reliable, stand-up witness. A blue-ribbon task force in Illinois has recommended that no death sentence be allowed in cases relying on the sole or primary word of jailhouse snitches. Such a reform in Ohio would commute the death penalty to life in prison for 10 Death Row inmates—all from Hamilton County.

The Hamilton County prosecutors' and attorney general's assumption of godlike qualities has created a conflict on the Sixth Circuit Court. As the *Washington Post* reported on November 12, "An angry dispute over capital punishment has erupted at a federal court in Ohio."

The *Post* recounted the bizarre events preceding Byrd's hearing and confirmed what *Columbus Alive* previously reported: That on September 11, 2001, amidst the chaos of the terrorist attacks, Montgomery attempted to get the

U.S. Supreme Court to lift Byrd's temporary stay of execution and proceed with his electrocution. Montgomery spokesperson Joe Case told the *Post*, "We were not aware of the gravity of the [attack] until later in the day. We had to do our job as enforcers of the law."

Left unexplained is how, early on, virtually every other person in the world was aware of the gravity of the attack. Perhaps Montgomery is not quite as infallible or omniscient as she suggests.

Whatever way Merz's report goes, one fact remains: The attorney general's attacks on the Ohio Public Defender's office are intended to have a chilling effect on the last line of defense for the poor and disproportionately minority Death Row inmates. If justice is to be served in Ohio, we have to admit that our state is no different than California or Virginia or Illinois. And those who act as if they have a private line directly to God and claim they never make mistakes must be seen for the bullies they are.

November 29, 2001

Request Denied

Federal Magistrate Michael R. Merz's 169-page Report and Recommendations regarding John W. Byrd Jr.'s claim of actual innocence was released last Friday, following an unprecedented evidentiary hearing ordered by a federal appeals court. Merz concluded that Byrd "has not proven to the level of clear and convincing evidence that he is actually innocent of the principal offender death specification of which he was convicted. Therefore his request to file a second federal habeas corpus petition should be denied."

Byrd is running out of possible ways to leave Death Row alive. "I'm probably screwed, but I'm going to keep fighting to the end," Byrd said during a telephone interview after Merz's opinion was released.

Byrd said he wasn't surprised by Merz's opinion. "Merz made it clear from the very beginning that he didn't view our case favorably," Byrd said. "He orchestrated the whole hearing to come out the way it did."

Merz may not believe there is "clear and convincing evidence" of Byrd's innocence, but there's never been any physical evidence of Byrd's guilt. He was convicted on the testimony of violent felon and jailhouse snitch Ronald Armstead, who was freed after an alleged deal with the prosecutors soon after Byrd's trial. At Byrd's hearing, jail inmate after jail inmate testified that Armstead told them he deliberately set Byrd up. This testimony was routinely dismissed by Merz in his report.

Merz got upset that the Ohio Public Defender's office failed to turn over three repetitious affidavits signed by John Brewer (in all the affidavits, two of which were properly turned over, Brewer repeatedly claimed that he, not Byrd, stabbed Monte Tewksbury). But the magistrate accepts without question the prosecution's failure to turn over far more important documents.

The most important missing document, Byrd said, was the transcript of Armstead's grand jury testimony, which the defense believed would show Armstead was acting as an agent of the state (something he denied at trial). Merz noted, "If permitted to file his new petition, Byrd intends to argue that the informers were planted by the prosecutors as forbidden in *Messiah v. United States.*" Merz accepted the Hamilton County prosecutors' explanation that the missing documents were either destroyed, lost or never existed in the first place.

"I've been told by someone in the Hamilton County prosecutor's office, who is disgusted with what is going on there, that the missing Armstead transcript was just recently destroyed," Byrd claimed.

Hamilton County Prosecutor Daniel Breyer conceded under oath that he brought Armstead and three other snitches from the jail to his office. Merz accepts Breyer's claim that Armstead, who was facing up to 15 years in prison on a parole revocation, was the only snitch who didn't ask for a deal.

The prosecutor said he independently acted as a good Samaritan when, after Armstead's testimony, Breyer quickly wrote a letter to the parole board which helped free Armstead.

Merz also cited Breyer's testimony as proof that Byrd stabbed Tewksbury. Breyer claims that Byrd's original trial attorney told the prosecutor he didn't want to put Byrd on the stand because the defendant might lie. The defense attorney says that conversation never took place. But Merz cites William Breyer's appellate briefs as evidence that Daniel Breyer is telling the truth. (William Breyer, who is handling the Byrd appeals for Hamilton County, is Daniel Breyer's brother.)

Merz's methodology is best displayed on page 70 of the report in the matter of the Pulsar watch. Allegedly, Byrd and his accomplices took a Pulsar watch from Tewksbury. But no Pulsar watch was produced by the prosecution at Byrd's original trial, nor has the prosecution produced an original copy of a police logbook showing Byrd wore such a watch.

Merz accepts without question the last-minute recollection of a deputy sheriff that Byrd was wearing a Pulsar watch. The prosecution didn't produce the Pulsar watch because it was "lost." That didn't stop Merz from writing in his opinion: "A Pulsar watch was taken from Byrd when he was booked into the jail and there is no testimony that Byrd usually wore such a watch."

Merz dismissed the testimony of defense witness Robert Pottinger, who signed an affidavit claiming that Byrd was not the knife-wielder at a second robbery later the night of Tewksbury's murder. The Ohio Supreme Court has deemed the circumstantial evidence suggesting that Byrd was the knife-wielder as "highly probative" and has used it to uphold his death sentence.

Pottinger's story, Merz said, "is not in the slightest bit credible," in part because Pottinger was drinking and had sex with Byrd's sister, Kim Hamer, and another woman the night before he signed an affidavit this summer.

According to the Associated Press, Pottinger acknowledged that he signed the affidavits shortly after he had sex with Hamer and another woman but was not promised sex in exchange for signing the documents.

More important, Pottinger was interviewed by *Columbus Alive* on August 28—before Hamer even talked to him—and Pottinger admitted to the same information later sworn to in the affidavit.

Byrd said the case against him has been corrupted "from Governor [Bob] Taft on down, because they want me to die. Taft's office was in almost constant contact with the assistant attorney generals handling the hearing."

Co-written with Martin Yant
December 6, 2001

Execution Showdown

A week before Christmas, the anti-death penalty movement received a huge present when a federal judge threw out the death penalty in a controversial case from the early 1980s; an affidavit signed by another man claimed he did the killing. The sentence of the Death Row inmate was commuted to life in prison.

No, we're not talking about Ohio's John W. Byrd Jr., but the internationally known Mumia Abu-Jamal.

The startling contrast between U.S. District Judge William Yohn's decision to remove Abu-Jamal from Death Row and federal Magistrate Michael R. Merz's bizarre opinion that Byrd's execution should proceed embodies everything that's wrong with the death penalty in the United States.

Abu-Jamal admitted being at the scene of the Philadelphia murder with a pistol; Hamilton County prosecutors admitted they had no murder weapon and no physical evidence tying Byrd to the Cincinnati convenience store murder scene.

In Abu-Jamal's case, his then-lawyers did not believe the confession of the other man; while in Byrd's case, his lawyers believed adamantly that John Brewer, not Byrd, was the killer. After all, the prosecutors and public defenders agreed that Brewer's footprint was on the store counter and the contents of the cash register were in his pocket. And Brewer confessed to the killing in no fewer than five affidavits dating back to the mid-'80s. Still, the vagaries of justice hold Abu-Jamal as a winner in the Death Row lottery, and Byrd's still praying for the justice jackpot.

In reality there were no winners and a lot of losers at Merz's hearing on Byrd's claim of actual innocence, a review of Merz's report shows. It's just the kind of report you'd expect from a Merz—Fred and Ethel Merz, that is.

The biggest loser of all in the case, the report makes clear, was Merz himself. The magistrate showed a clear bias against Byrd and the anti-death penalty contingent that opposes Byrd's execution.

On page 58 of the report, Merz wrote: "Yesterday it was brought to my attention that a person claiming to be a press representative was in the courtroom, purporting to represent the *Columbus Free Press*. The only thing I could find about the *Columbus Free Press* on the web was something on a Romanian website this morning. When challenged by the marshal for press credentials, she could not produce press credentials."

Merz mentions in a footnote that the person in question, Ida Strong, later "faxed the marshal what purported to be *Columbus Free Press* credentials signed on behalf of that paper by Bob Fitrakis, a person heavily involved in covering this case for *Columbus Alive*," as if this was some kind of sin.

Of course, Strong was covering the trial for the *Free Press*, a newspaper published since 1970 and one of the first alternative papers to establish a website in 1996. A Google search for "Columbus Free Press" turned up 1,190 hits. The very first hit stated, "The *Columbus Free Press* is a progressive newspaper and website devoted to reporting on social justice issues." The level of Merz's Internet research skills are on par with his legal analysis. Romania, indeed.

Based on these foolish, off-the-record allegations and erroneous-to-the-point-of-absurdity web searches, Merz stated that Strong might be cited for contempt of court for unspecified reasons. Merz went on to state, "Several courtroom personnel observed her visibly signaling to Mr. Hall [a witness] when he was on the stand before she was removed from the jury box." Merz also stated that Dan Cahill, a listed Byrd witness, probably would not be permitted to testify because he was seen having lunch with Strong.

Strong sent the *Free Press* reports from the first two days of the trial before she was threatened with contempt of court. She wrote: "During the hearing, Roger Hall was called as a witness. He was one of the prisoners who I campaigned for his release from the supermax [prison] months before. Roger must have recognized me from one of my pictures, which had appeared either in a newsletter or on the news. After testifying...he looked over at me and held his hand up... I in return held my hand up in a show of acknowledgement to him. That's all I did was acknowledge Roger Hall."

Cahill claims that Alan Johnson of the *Columbus Dispatch* talked to him for over a half hour and the judge didn't threaten Johnson with contempt. Merz's approach to the First Amendment appears as misguided as his handling of death penalty cases.

The Ohio Public Defender's office also came off poorly—and not just because of the last-minute surfacing of three additional affidavits signed by Brewer, who claims he committed the 1983 murder for which Byrd was sentenced to die.

Merz noted that the public defenders made a major argument out of Assistant Hamilton County Prosecutor William Breyer's statement that jailhouse snitch Ronald Armstead had testified before the grand jury, even though a transcript of his testimony could not be located. "Despite the inflated rhetoric" about compelling Breyer to testify, Merz noted, Byrd's attorney never called him to the stand.

That seemed typical of the public defenders' mishandling of Byrd's case over the years, as Merz demonstrated with other examples. The public defenders also seemed to have done a bad job preparing their witnesses. Brewer, by far the most crucial, clearly irritated Merz with his arrogant demeanor. Although what actual influence the public defenders had over Brewer, linked in government documents to the leadership of the racist Aryan Brotherhood, is another issue.

The assistant state attorneys general performed no better, as they diverted attention from the lack of evidence of Byrd's guilt by creating a sideshow over the public defenders' gaffes.

Still, as we celebrate the holidays, there are some small wins for anti-death penalty advocates in Ohio. On December 12, 2001, 50 central Ohio ministers and religious leaders called for a moratorium on capital punishment at an Interfaith Coalition to Stop Executions press conference. Seven days later, Cincinnati City Council, by a 7-2 vote, passed a resolution calling for a death penalty moratorium. While the resolution isn't legally binding, it at least sends a strong pro-justice signal from Ohio's most death penalty-happy county.

Co-written with Martin Yant
December 27, 2001

Still Looking For
"The Truth"

"You know the truth." That's what Robert Pottinger told Kim Hamer, John W. Byrd's sister, in a tape recorded conversation as she pleaded with Pottinger to help keep her brother from being executed for the 1983 murder of Monte Tewksbury.

Pottinger later agreed to sign an affidavit that said he, not Byrd, participated in a second robbery the night of Tewksbury's death. Byrd is scheduled to be executed for Tewksbury's murder on February 19, 2002.

Pottinger testified at an November 2001 hearing before Federal Magistrate Michael R. Merz that he committed the second robbery because Byrd had passed out in the truck they were using. In his opinion denying Byrd's claim of "actual innocence," based on the testimony of Pottinger and others, Merz said Pottinger's story "is not in the slightest bit credible" and that "he hints at such an admission in his taped conversation with Kim Hamer when he tells her she knows what the truth is."

You might add judges to the saying that the only time most cops get exercise is when they jump to conclusions. Merz clearly jumped to the wrong conclusion that "the truth" Pottinger spoke of was that Byrd killed Tewksbury.

The truth Pottinger actually referred to was the admission he made to Hamer that he, not Byrd, participated in the first robbery as well as the second, according to Hamer.

Pottinger admitted to *Columbus Alive* that, while partying with friends in the 1980s, he bragged about being the killer. But Pottinger specifically told *Alive* he did not murder Tewksbury and he expressed concern about being charged with the crime.

Byrd has always avoided talking about Pottinger's full role in the robberies. Byrd, John Brewer (who claims he killed Tewksbury) and Danny Woodall—the three accomplices arrested and charged with Tewksbury's murder after Pottinger had run from the truck—allegedly agreed not to discuss Pottinger's involvement, and they always kept their word.

Byrd remained circumspect when he was asked about Pottinger in an interview last week, less than a month before his scheduled execution.

"You know what the truth is," Byrd said, echoing Pottinger. "Just look at the evidence. Tewksbury said the guy who stabbed him was wearing a plaid shirt, and the investigator's notes say who always wore plaid shirts [Pottinger]."

Pottinger testified that Byrd was passed out in the truck during the second robbery. Asked if he was passed out in the truck during the first robbery as well, Byrd said: "I imagine." He added, however, that it was hard for him to remember when he was awake and when he wasn't because he was so drunk that night.

Did you go into the first store? he was asked.

"I never went in any store," Byrd replied. "That's what people have to look at. There's never been [any] evidence to place me at this crime—never."

A source in the Ohio Public Defender's office disclosed to *Alive* prior to the Merz hearing that John Brewer alluded to Pottinger's involvement and the crucial "plaid shirt" in the first robbery. According to the source, "Brewer said, 'Who do the police say was wearing the plaid shirts? What did the guy who was killed say about the plaid shirt? How stupid are people?'"

With so many questions remaining in the Byrd case and no physical evidence linking him to the murder, Byrd asked the governor in a January 22, 2002, letter not "to grant me clemency" but "to grant a reprieve and request for a federal investigation into my conviction."

No eyewitnesses have ever identified Byrd as the actual killer; the physical evidence points to Brewer, who has admitted in five affidavits since 1988 that he stabbed Tewksbury.

The sole direct evidence against Byrd is the testimony of Ronald Armstead, a notorious Hamilton County snitch, and fellow inmate Virgil Jordan. In an October 24, 2001, court order, Merz greatly limited Byrd's request for documents from the Cincinnati Police Department and the Hamilton County Sheriff. Merz refused to consider any documents from 1983, the actual time period when Byrd, Armstead and Jordan were in the Hamilton County workhouse together and when Byrd's confession allegedly took place.

Oddly, Merz reasoned that "All documents related to Virgil Jordan and Ronald Armstead" need not be produced because the documents were too voluminous.

The public defender's office was unable to obtain records that would show whether or not Armstead testified before the Hamilton County grand jury that indicted Byrd; Jordan did testify before the grand jury and at Brewer's trial. Merz's ruling thwarted the exploration of the possibility that Jordan and Armstead conspired to fabricate testimony against Byrd.

Neither Armstead nor Jordan testified at the Merz hearing. Armstead could not be located, though he was last reported to be working on an Alaskan cruise ship; Jordan died last summer of a drug overdose.

Merz declined to review Jordan's Department of Rehabilitation and Corrections records as part of the hearing, ruling they were "Too remote from the central controversy before the court." While Armstead played the key role of Byrd's accuser in court, the record establishes that it was Jordan's grand jury testimony that resulted in capital charges being brought against Byrd.

Moreover, Merz shielded from scrutiny police documents showing Armstead's and Jordan's roles as law enforcement informers. Carl Vollman, Byrd's lead prosecutor, had previously utilized Jordan as an informant and grand jury witness in a murder trial. There are 10 people on Ohio's Death Row convicted primarily or solely on the word of a snitch—all 10 are from Hamilton County.

Merz also denied requests for subpoenas revealing Jordan's and Armstead's roles as informants for the FBI, the DEA and the defunct Regional Enforcement Narcotics Unit. Merz ruled once again that Armstead's and Jordan's long histories as snitches were "too remote from the central controversy."

Jordan's brother Watson and his sister Doris both acknowledge in signed affidavits that their brother is a well-known "snitch." Watson Jordan stated in his affidavit,

"He [Virgil] usually gets out of his legal trouble by snitching on people. In the past, Virgil would get arrested and be put in jail. Soon after, he would return home. I thought it was strange that he got out so soon and figured he'd snitched for the police... In the early 1980s, Virgil went undercover as a city trash collector. He used the alias Michael Stokes. The city used him to catch city workers using and selling drugs."

Doris Jordan swears that "Virgil is a big liar. When he gets into legal trouble, he'll lie to get out of it. He would set you up in a minute if it helped him."

Co-written with Martin Yant
January 31, 2002

Last-Minute Pleas

John W. Byrd Jr. continues to fight for his life as his February 19, 2002, execution date rapidly approaches. On Friday, February 1, Byrd managed to telephone this reporter to explain the mounting tension and bizarre rituals brewing inside the Mansfield Correctional Institution.

Byrd is under a suicide watch to make sure he doesn't cheat the state of its well-scripted execution. Social workers and medical personnel are working with Byrd to ensure he'll be healthy when he's put to death.

Byrd told *Alive* he believes he should get a "reprieve" until there's a federal investigation into his allegations of widespread corruption in the Hamilton County Prosecutor's office. "They're trying to kill me, brother, before anyone can take a close look at what they do," Byrd said.

On Monday, Byrd sent to *Alive* an audio tape of a phone call he made from Death Row alleging that anytime "I speak about the governor [with reporters], interviews will be terminated." Byrd made an appeal to Ohio voters to remember his case in November, and asked that they support his "First Amendment rights" prior to his execution.

Byrd's desperate pleas for a reprieve appear to be falling upon the deaf ears of Bob Taft. But the emotions stirred by the case remain indelibly etched in court records.

In a ringing dissent, joined by four other Sixth Circuit U.S. Court of Appeals judges, Judge Nathaniel R. Jones wrote: "The Court majority certifies a death sentence that the state of Ohio secured in contravention of the fundamental imperatives of our constitutional order."

Judge Jones summed up the facts of the Byrd case this way: "No eyewitness or other physical evidence identifies the particular robber responsible for the murder, and the only evidence distinguishing the assailants are the representations of a jailhouse 'snitch.'"

Jones argued in his dissent that the only reason anyone believed Ronald Armstead, the "snitch," is because the prosecutor "vouched" for his credibility: "Such prosecutory testimony on the credibility of a witness is undoubtedly unconstitutional, and in a case that turns on the veracity of that witness—a jailhouse snitch no less—the error is prejudicial."

Byrd hopes the U.S. Supreme Court will closely consider Jones' dissent in his expected last-minute appeal. In a January 22, 2002, letter to Governor Taft, Byrd raised a variety of concerns that he wanted a federal investigation to probe.

"There is no evidence that places me inside the crime scene. [Neither] my fingerprints nor shoeprints were found at [the] scene nor on anything. My hair was not found in any of the masks. I don't fit any of the descriptions given. My conviction is based on perjured testimony the prosecution knew was perjured and have been doing a[n] effective job of concealing ever since," Byrd wrote the governor.

In his *Alive* interview last week, Byrd said, "It must be hard on you knowing I'm telling the truth about the evidence."

In both his letter to the governor, Byrd pointed to the strange role of the Breyer brothers in his case. Byrd vehemently complained about the fact that Daniel Breyer was the trial prosecutor in his case and his brother William Breyer remains the Hamilton County post-conviction prosecutor in his case.

"William Breyer has been covering up for his brother for many years now. It must be a wonderful thing to be from a county where it is common practice for the post-conviction prosecutor to author the finding of facts and the conclusions of law for the post-conviction judge to accept in toto, knowing full well all other following courts will accept this finding as well," Byrd wrote.

Byrd's letter urges the governor to look at "the evidence." Byrd stresses the following facts in his request for a reprieve:

• "The two supposed specks of blood found on my pant leg was not that of Montes Tewksbury... Mr. Tewksbury's blood did *not* contain the H antigen! Nineteen years ago this finding would have been [treated] as any DNA testing performed today."

• "The only physical evidence the state tried to use was that I had a watch that *could* have been Mr. Tewksbury's. However at trial this [watch] couldn't be produced."

• "Breyer and [Carl] Vollman knowingly solicited perjured testimony from Armstead and in turn vouched for his credibility."

• "Not only did Armstead get out, but he was flown to [California]. Prosecutors have said that Armstead's mother had paid for this plane ticket...This simply is not true. Mrs. Armstead has denied paying for any such ticket."

"Once I am murdered life cannot be placed back into my

body. The system shouldn't be permitted to protect itself against what it has done to me at the expense of my life," Byrd wrote. "Murdering me will not make this ugly chapter in Ohio's history go away."

February 7, 2002

"The Wrong Man"

From rural Mennonites to a large contingent of Kenyon College students, more than the usual suspects chanted "John Byrd—the wrong man" on Parkview Avenue in Bexley last Saturday.

The 300 or so anti-death penalty activists demonstrating at Governor Bob Taft's mansion indicates a growing death penalty abolition movement in Ohio. The pending February 19, 2002, execution of Byrd appears to be the catalyst behind the increasingly vocal protest. Unlike the recent Wilford Berry and Jay D. Scott executions, death penalty foes vehemently argue that with Byrd, the state is about to execute "the wrong man." The case has even attracted the attention of Bianca Jagger of Amnesty International, who was in Columbus this week on Byrd's behalf.

In court documents, Hamilton County prosecutors and the attorney general's office concede that their only direct evidence against Byrd rests on the testimony of the now-missing notorious jailhouse snitch Ronald Armstead.

In fact, in the past the state has fought attempts by Byrd to have two small specks of blood on his clothes tested to see if it matches the victim. Instead, as court records reveal, the prosecutors maintain that Byrd's guilt centers around the controversial testimony of Armstead. A violent felon and known heroin addict, Armstead was facing up to 15 years in prison when he emerged as Hamilton County prosecutors' star witness in the 1983 Byrd trial.

Former Cincinnati Congressman Thomas Luken was instrumental in convincing Cincinnati City Council to pass a resolution last December calling on the Ohio General Assembly to support "a moratorium on the imposition of the death penalty in the state of Ohio until a fair and impartial review of the application of the death penalty is conducted."

"Byrd just can't get a break. He loses by one vote—four to three—at the Ohio Supreme Court, and then loses by one vote at the Court of Appeals," Luken told *Columbus Alive*. "The most important thing people in Ohio can do is go to their local governments and have them pass resolutions calling for a moratorium on the death penalty."

Byrd has asked the governor not for clemency, but to simply stay his execution pending a federal investigation into his case. Byrd recently told *Alive* he doesn't trust a state probe. "The Hamilton County prosecutors, the attorney general, the prison officials and the governor's office have all been working together to make sure the truth doesn't come out," he said.

The Ohio Supreme Court, by that four-to-three vote, denied Byrd a new trial based on the notion that Byrd was at a second robbery the night of Tewksbury's murder. The robbers wore masks and tests on hair found in the masks proved inconclusive as to who wore them. But this did not stop prosecutors from arguing to the Ohio Supreme Court that it was Byrd's hair, even though he did not match the physical description of the robber. Improvements in the accuracy of DNA testing now, 18 years later, could prove

Byrd's guilt or innocence. Death penalty foes are outraged that the governor steadfastly refuses to consider Byrd's request to re-test the hair or blood evidence.

The Cincinnati City Council resolution noted, "The advent of DNA testing has already caused an increase in exoneration of condemned persons and those convicted of murder."

The same year Byrd was convicted, Canada witnessed a similarly spectacular wrongful conviction case. Like Byrd, Guy Paul Morin was convicted of murder on what turned out to be the phony testimony of two jailhouse informants; Morin was exonerated when he was granted a new trial and proven innocent by DNA tests. Canada since established new guidelines on jailhouse snitches. Before one can testify, the informant must appear before a screening committee and prove that his or her story can be corroborated by someone other than another inmate.

Byrd's prosecutors have successfully fought any discovery attempts that would reveal Armstead's extensive history of snitching for the Cincinnati police, Hamilton County prosecutors, the DEA and the FBI.

Democratic gubernatorial candidate Tim Hagan last week told OSU law school students, "The death penalty is barbaric."

"We are the only industrial country with the death penalty. Society does not make itself greater by practicing the thing we hate," Hagan said, referring to murder. "If I was governor I wouldn't sign a death warrant... A just society does not make that kind of arbitrary decision."

The Cincinnati City Council resolution stated, "Ohio Supreme Court Justice Paul Pfeifer, a sponsor of Ohio's 1981 death penalty law, now says that he is personally 'moving closer to opposing the death penalty and that an independent panel should review the cases of the 203 Death Row inmates'" in Ohio.

The Republican governor of Illinois already halted all executions in that state, proclaiming the death penalty system is "broken."

The new abolitionist movement is apparently causing concern in law enforcement circles. Following the largest demonstration yet at the governor's mansion, a spokesperson for the Ohio State Troopers told Ohio News Network that they were increasing security at the governor's mansion and his office from now until Byrd's execution date.

February 14, 2002

Infamous Last Words

Twenty-two hours before the state strapped John Byrd Jr. onto a gurney and pumped poison into his veins, he gave an hour-long dying declaration to his family's attorney, Clifford Arnebeck. Although he was unwilling to finger Bobby Pottinger in the nearly 19 years he was incarcerated on Death Row, Byrd's final confession offered new information pointing to Pottinger's involvement in a second robbery on the night of the 1983 stabbing death of King Kwik convenience store clerk Monte Tewksbury.

Byrd alleged that Pottinger left the scene of the second robbery with the "missing" contents of the cash register in his pocket.

Cincinnati police records indicate that the then-17-year-old Pottinger, who was not eligible for the death penalty, was the initial murder suspect in the Tewksbury slaying. A police informant had identified Pottinger as the mystery man in the plaid or black-and-red shirt described by both Tewksbury and eyewitnesses at the second robbery. Investigatory files relating to the case indicate that, following Tewksbury's murder, Pottinger immediately fled the Cincinnati area for Florida.

According to the prosecutors' version of events, Pottinger spent the entire day of Tewksbury's murder with the trio of accomplices who robbed the King Kwik store; John Brewer, William Woodall and John Byrd dropped Pottinger off at his home before the robbery. The trio then, according to prosecutors, returned to Pottinger's house to pick him up again before robbing a second convenience store, U-Tote-Em. Pottinger agreed to testify for the prosecution but was later declared a hostile witness after accusing the prosecution of putting words in his mouth.

Pottinger has sworn under oath that he was the second robber at the U-Tote-Em store and admitted to *Columbus Alive* that he bragged about killing Tewksbury, although Pottinger denies the actual killing. The emergence of Pottinger in Byrd's dying declaration may help explain why Byrd, who always claimed to be drunk and drugged out during the robberies, never matched the descriptions provided by eyewitnesses.

The most bizarre aspect of the Byrd case remains how the Hamilton County Prosecutor's office chose to prosecute Byrd as the actual killer of Tewksbury when the prosecutors admitted in pleading after pleading that they have no direct physical evidence against Byrd, other than the word of notorious jailhouse snitch Ronald Armstead.

"My co-defendant and his sister were working, Johnny [Brewer] and Debbie [Brewer], together with the prosecutor's office," to plant the idea that Byrd was the killer, Byrd insisted. Evidence uncovered by *Alive* indicates that Debbie Brewer was serving as an informant for local law enforcement authorities at the time of her brother's arrest.

Ohio Public Defender David Bodiker speculates that Debbie Brewer's role as a police informant may have bought her brother special treatment regarding the capital indictment.

Byrd admitted to "a little too much drinking and a little too much drugging" on the day of Tewksbury's murder and "waking up into a nightmare." He stressed that the detectives let him sleep off his substance abuse for nine hours before even questioning him about the case.

He claimed the prosecutors knew he didn't stab Tewksbury, but they initially approached him with a deal: He would only serve 10 years in prison for pleading guilty to murder and testifying that John Brewer was the killer (Brewer's footprint was on the King Kwik counter and the contents of the cash register allegedly in his pocket). Byrd said, "They told me that three people were arrested, three would be convicted. Which side are you going to fall on?"

When he refused to perjure himself or "recall" facts he didn't remember through the booze and drug haze of the robbery night, Byrd contended, prosecutors sought the death penalty for him instead of Brewer. Byrd maintained that "a careful review of the evidence"—which did not occur at his original trial—will clear him posthumously.

During the hour-long dying declaration, Byrd reiterated the long list of inconsistencies in the case, pointing to the fact that shoe prints, hair samples and fingerprints as well as blood tests provided no direct evidence linking him to the murder. "I'm not afraid of DNA tests," Byrd stated, raising the specter of a posthumous civil trial that may prove prosecutors wrong. In past criminal proceedings, the prosecution has resisted attempts by Byrd's attorneys to test two specks of blood evidence found on Byrd's pants.

Byrd described himself as "just one of the white guys that didn't mix with black guys" in the Hamilton County jail in 1983. "It was all segregated off. Why would I approach someone I didn't know [Armstead, who is black] and admit murder?" Byrd asked.

Byrd called his recent hearing before Federal Magistrate Michael R. Merz a "farce." "Merz let us know that he thought the whole proceeding was full of crap. He didn't uphold the orders of the Sixth Circuit [Court of Appeals] or his own oath," Byrd said. Byrd particularly singled out Merz's decision to limit and deny evidence regarding the use of snitches by the Hamilton County Prosecutor's office.

Maintaining to the end that he did not kill Tewksbury, Byrd declared, "I will not bow to no man." Quoting the words of Jesus, he said of the state officials putting him to death, "Forgive them father, for they don't know what they do."

"May God guide their hearts, and correct this wrong to the best of their ability. They cannot continue to murder people they way they do, to enhance their own careers," Byrd said. "Capital punishment is not the will of God."

Byrd swore in an affidavit that he was innocent in the death of Tewksbury. If Arnebeck has his way, a wrongful death suit will give John Byrd the hearing on the evidence he never got at his original trial and answer some of the questions about the strange conduct of the Hamilton County Prosecutor's office.

February 28, 2002

Death Row Turns Healers Into Killers

This month they packed up "Old Sparky," Ohio's electric chair, and shipped it off to the state's historical society. Just as the guillotine was banished to museums, electrocution, like beheading before it, is now part of our barbaric past.

Now we have the supposedly more-humane lethal injection. But local physician Jonathon I. Groner argues, "Lethal injection is turning healers into killers." In an interview with *Columbus Alive*, Groner expressed concern that "the aura of humanity surrounding lethal injection is enhanced by treating the inmate as a patient."

In a draft of a paper Groner's writing, "Lethal Injection: A Stain on the Face of Medicine," he points out that 65 years ago Germany's Nazi government "encouraged physicians to become direct participants in state-sponsored killings."

"The national 'euthanasia' program, code name 'T-4,' was initiated in 1939 by Adolf Hitler for the purpose of killing physically and mentally handicapped patients," Groner writes. "In the words of T-4's chief administrator, 'The syringe belongs in the hand of the physician.'"

Roger J. Lifton points out in his book, *The Nazi Doctors*,

"The imagery of killing in the name of healing" and the "medicalization" of state-sanctioned murder was a key feature of the Third Reich.

The Nazi killings were ideologically motivated to enhance the so-called "master race" and, in the name of law and order, eventually expanded to kill some 6,000 non-Jewish German children. Among their crimes included "bed-wetting, pimples, a swarthy complexion or even annoying the nurse," H.G. Gallagher documents in *By Trust Betrayed: Patients, Physicians and the License to Kill in the Third Reich.*

Groner reflects on this history in his writings, but notes that in the United States the medicalization of death is driven by a different ideology—corporate capitalism's propensity for efficiency and "cost containment." As former governor and current Senator George Voinovich used to say, "Doing more with less."

"During the execution moratorium of the early 1970s, Oklahoma's unused electric chair deteriorated so severely that $60,000 in repairs were required to make it functional again," Groner writes. "Unwilling to spend this sum on condemned prisoners, an Oklahoma state senator consulted the Department of Anesthesiology at the University of Oklahoma searching for medications that might do the electric chair's work."

Dr. Stanley Deutsch, a professor and practicing anesthesiologist, came up with the solution: "Using a barbiturate followed by a muscle relaxant would be an ideal (and inexpensive) way to bring about a speedy and humane demise." Deutsch's recommendation became Oklahoma law in 1978, but it was neighboring Texas that killed the first person by modern lethal injection in 1982. By 1999, 95 percent of all executions were carried out by injection.

Since 1982, there has been a 50-fold increase in the annual number of executions in the U.S. Groner argues that this is directly tied to the medicalization of executions. "The medical profession is the last holdout" that's propping up the execution system, in Groner's opinion.

But physician participation in executions is "specifically condemned" by the American Medical Association. The AMA's Council on Ethical and Judicial Affairs states that a physician "should not be a participant in a legally author-ized execution." The AMA outlines eight specific practices that constitute "direct participation," including injecting lethal drugs, inspecting or maintaining injection devices, ordering lethal drugs, selecting IV sites, monitoring vital signs and pronouncing a prisoner's death, Groner explained.

Groner recently made a public records request to the Ohio Rehabilitation and Corrections Department and the prison at Lucasville to determine physicians' involvement in Ohio's execution protocol.

"If medical societies [including the AMA] do not con-demn physician participation in lethal injection," Groner writes, "then physicians in the United States are destined to become like the 'euthanasia' doctors of Nazi Germany who were instrumental in that government's program to execute physically and mentally disabled patients."

A popular book in Nazi Germany, titled *The Permission to Destroy Life Unworthy of Life*, articulated the duty of physi-cians to assist the state in removing "human ballast" and "empty shells of human beings." Medical ethics required that "less valuable members of society had to be abandoned and pushed out."

In Groner's analysis, Death Row is filled with the same type of "human ballast." Groner points to "the poor, the poorly represented, the innocent and the mentally ill and mentally retarded" that occupy Death Row in the U.S. "More than 10 percent of Death Row inmates suffer from mental illness, and at least 10 percent are mentally retarded... Thirty-five mentally retarded people have been executed since 1976," Groner writes.

While Groner concedes that the analogy between "death camps" and Death Row may sound far-fetched, "extreme transmissions" often shed light on more subtle moral dilemmas, he argues. At Nuremberg, the doctor in charge of the T-4 program adamantly defended with "the deepest convictions" Germany's lethal injections. The director argued, "It was never meant to be murder" and "death can mean deliverance."

Ohio Public Radio reporter Bill Cohen, who witnessed John Byrd's recent execution, described Byrd's lethal injection death as "peaceful." Governor Bob Taft spoke of the "healing" and "closure" resulting from Byrd's killing. The governor acknowledged that he had prayed to God for guidance and uttered the phrase "God bless the Tewksbury family" in condemning Byrd and attempting to cure our state from evil.

March 21, 2002

Human Rights Violations

By the time you read this, it's likely that Death Row inmate Alton Coleman, who went on a killing spree in the 1980s, will have been executed. I spoke with Michael Manley, Columbus' Amnesty International Coordinator, who told me he was working on a report to the United Nations Human Rights Committee documenting violations in Ohio regarding executions.

The human rights violations against the first three men executed here since the reinstatement of the death penalty were easy enough to guess. Let's see, Wilford Berry was mentally retarded and brain damaged. He refused his lawyers' attempts to defend him. I can't find any other country that readily admits to killing someone in Berry's condition.

Next, Jay D. Scott was a well-documented lifelong schizophrenic. There's a handful of rogue nations that would have done him in.

The third, John Byrd, was convicted without any direct evidence against him except the word of a jailhouse snitch. Other than the Third Reich under Hitler, and the state of Texas, only Ohio is willing to kill in that situation.

Manley also mentioned the death of Coleman as a

human rights violation. Manley stresses that Coleman suffered from fetal alcohol syndrome, that his brain and nervous system were damaged at birth from his mother's excessive drinking. Once he was born, his mother, a known prostitute, alcoholic and drug abuser, threw him in a garbage can. Throughout his childhood, he was abused physically and sexually.

Manley argues that Coleman's execution accomplishes nothing for our society; when we allow the Alton Colemans of the world to be raised in such abject poverty and such a vicious environment, we reap what we sow. The political spin of the day is how all these executions will heal the families of the victims. When will Ohio's politicians ever seek to heal the young children immersed in poverty who are the future Alton Colemans?

April 25, 2002

Axis Of Injustice

The rogue state of Ohio and its axis of injustice is at it again. The "axis" of Attorney General Betty Montgomery's office, Ohio prosecutors who refuse to follow the law and Governor Bob Taft's office are conspiring to execute Greg Lott on August 27, despite Lott's IQ of 72.

In June the U.S. Supreme Court reversed a 1989 decision and ruled that the Constitution bars execution of the mentally retarded. The American Psychiatric Association's *Diagnostic and Statistical Manual of Mental Disorders* establishes individuals with IQs between 70 and 75 who exhibit significant deficits in adaptive behavior as "mentally retarded."

Despite Lott's score of 72 on a test administered by the Ohio Department of Rehabilitation and Corrections in 1986, Ohio's axis, in the tradition of World War II's fascist axis powers, are dedicated to executing the mentally retarded.

University of Cincinnati professor Howard Tolley, a human rights expert, points out that the recent Supreme Court decision leaves it up to each state to determine the procedure for establishing who on Death Row is mentally retarded. The Supreme Court's decision quoted a psychiatric text noting: "It is estimated that between one and three percent of the population has an IQ between 70 and 75 or lower."

Because the Supreme Court's (now-overturned) 1989 decision made the United States the only democracy in the world willing to kill the mentally retarded, Lott's low IQ has never been reviewed on appeal by any court. Lott's current counsel, Joe Bodine, has two appeals pending before the Ohio Supreme Court, with his client's IQ in the mentally retarded range being perhaps his last best hope.

One would think that Taft would be shamed into commuting Lott's sentence to life in prison, but the blueblood is hell-bent for political reasons on making Ohio the North's only yahoo-style Texas justice state. Let's look at the governor's record: In Ohio's first four executions since the death penalty was reinstated, with the fifth to follow within two weeks, the guv signed off to kill the mentally retarded and brain damaged so-called "volunteer" Wilford Berry, one of God's most pathetic creatures; next was life-long schizophrenic Jay D. Scott; and the third was on Death Row only because of the word of a junkie snitch, despite strong claims of actual innocence.

On the race issue alone, Governor Rich White Guy is showing his true colors. Since the death penalty was reinstated in the U.S. in 1976, there's been 172 blacks executed for killing whites, and only 12 whites executed for killing blacks. Three out of the four already executed in Ohio killed white victims. Despite a U.S. Sixth Circuit Court of Appeals decision stating Lott's victim's race as black, Tolley reports that Bodine checked the autopsy report and original pleadings that indicate that Lott's victim was white.

This would mean that if the mentally retarded Lott is executed on August 27, 80 percent of those executed in Ohio killed white victims and three out of the five, or 60 percent, of those executed were black. To compound matters, 87 of Ohio's 88 county prosecutors are white and there are no African-American justices on Ohio's Supreme Court.

As usual in Ohio, the prosecution withheld evidence in the Lott case that is required by law to be turned over to the defense. The victim, John McGrath, remained alive for a week after being tied up and burned during a burglary. Detective reports indicated that McGrath could not identify a sketch of Lott as his assailant. Also, the prosecutor argued that Lott had deliberately carried with him a bottle of lamp oil to burn McGrath to death, thus establishing premeditation, a requirement for capital murder in Ohio. Another police report indicating that there was an oil lamp in McGrath's house was never turned over to the defense either.

The prosecutor's failure to turn over obviously exculpatory evidence to the defense counsel is blatantly illegal and, as Tolley points out, "In 10 other cases, Ohio's appellate courts have criticized misconduct by the same assistant prosecutor who conducted Lott's trial."

In short, in the rogue state of Ohio, county prosecutors know they can clearly violate the well-established rules that require the disclosure of all exculpatory evidence. The axis of injustice encourages its prosecutors to cheat in death penalty cases. Don't worry, the attorney general and governor will cover up for you.

While other states like Illinois and Maryland have instituted moratoriums on executions, accepting that the death penalty system is broken and needs to be reviewed, Ohio's axis of injustice is dedicated to joining a few rogue states worldwide in killing the mentally retarded. No other Western democracy would even consider killing Lott.

As Tolley argues, "Greg Lott's execution will not make Ohio safer and would be an unjust exercise of state power. Ohio experienced 630 murders in 1987 but sentenced only Greg Lott and nine other men to Death Row in the period. Mr. Lott is typical of the very few individuals that Ohio selects for execution—a poor, black, male of unsound mind with inadequate counsel defending against state prosecutors who use improper methods."

August 15, 2002

The Last Mile

BY JOHN WILLIAM BYRD JR.

Sunday, March 13, 1994, at 12:35 p.m., exactly 35 hours and 25 minutes before my scheduled state-sanctioned murder, the "Death Row Escort Squad" arrived at my cell, saying, "It's time, Byrd Dog."

"Strip," said one. A number of men stood in front of my cell, nervously watching as I shed my clothing, perhaps for the last "strip search" of my life. After going through the usual routine of "lift 'em and spread 'em," I got dressed, backed up to the cell door, and was handcuffed.

While this was going on, an eerie silence had settled over the entire cellblock. There was none of the usual boisterous yelling, laughter, loud radios or TVs playing. Nothing—complete silence. Then, as I backed out of my cell and started on that long walk, the cellblock erupted into a cacophonous uproar: "Stay strong," "good luck," the voices yelled out to me. As I bid them farewell, I vowed, "I'll represent us *all* well, no matter what happens. Stay strong," meaning that I would not grovel and whine, as some involved in the process would like to see.

Along the way, as I walked down the long main corridor, loud voices raised in solidarity and encouragement greeted me as I passed each cellblock. The shouts from the

233

cellblocks caused my escorts, and the numerous guards that lined the corridor to become alarmed, the fear and terror of the past riot still fresh in their memories. In an effort to make me speed up the leisurely pace I had assumed, meeting each and every eye along the way, they started walking faster. I maintained my stride, and soon they slowed down, resigned to the pace I had set.

Upon arriving in J-1 Supermax, I was once again strip-searched and my regular Death Row clothing was exchanged for Death House clothing. "Odd," I thought to myself. "What difference does what one is wearing have on the fact of one's impending death?!"

The atmosphere of the Death House was smothering, suffocating, as if there were a shortage of oxygen. Everyone moved as if in slow motion. Their every move seeming to have been thoroughly rehearsed, learned, robot-like professionalism, as now, for the first time in over 30 years, they, the elite Death Squad, had been called upon to commit murder in the name of the state of Ohio. In some of their eyes I saw fear, concern and revulsion—in others, sadistic glee. Looking at each one of them with steady, unblinking eyes, I sized them up individually.

Shortly after entering the death cell proper, my attorneys arrived to inform me as to the current state of my situation. We discussed this at great length, and I felt confident that everything possible was being done to halt the insidious plot to murder me that had been set into motion by the state of Ohio.

After enjoying the time spent with my lawyers, I immediately contacted my woman and, later, other family members, on the phone that had been provided. I attempted as best I could to assuage their worries and fears. With each

one I tried to explain the situation, based on my knowledge and information provided to me by my lawyers. This
was very difficult, given the fact that they all were well
aware of the appeal process and knew this latest attempt by
the state of Ohio to murder me was simply a political move,
and not based upon law. I still wanted to calm their fears,
give them strength, and assure them all that everything was
under control, and my lawyers were on top of everything—every move the state was trying to make.

For the most part I remained in constant contact with
my woman and family by phone, and was permitted to
have a couple short visits with my lovely woman, engaging
in spirited conversation with some of the people who had
come down from the Ohio Public Defender's Office, and
was truly touched by them.

At times, there were periods when time seemed to stand
still, then suddenly speed up. I was offered food, but
refused to eat, fearing that it may have been "doctored up"
with drugs to make me less resistant and responsive. This
refusal was not based on some unreasonable paranoia, but
through years of incarceration I know firsthand just how
devious prison officials can be, and I wasn't about to take
any chances!

The whirlwind of activity continued around me, and as
night approached, there was no thought of sleep in my
mind. Throughout the night I was on the phone talking to
people I haven't heard from in years. Everyone expressing
their support, love, concern and pledging their assistance.

Monday morning, March 14, 1994, was indeed a "blue
Monday" for us all as we learned of the apparent unprecedented and mean-spirited tactics being employed by the
"honorable" Carl Rubin, the judge assigned to my case. It

seems that even though he had my writ of habeas corpus and motion for a stay of execution before him since March 7, he decided to wait until the "11th hour" before making a ruling, knowing full well that the situation was critical, and time was of the essence.

An example of the insidious plot he had hatched in his muddled mind began when he instructed two of my attorneys to meet in his chambers at noon. At the conclusion of the meeting, he informed my attorneys that he would deny my motion for a stay of execution, and that he would issue his ruling at approximately 3 p.m.—nine hours before my scheduled execution! He made this ruling with full knowledge that it was legally wrong, but in keeping with his own "personal" feelings about the length of time my appeal was taking. As he stated on one occasion, "There comes a time when all of this must come to an end."

Now he had appointed himself the Supreme Litigator— usurping the power of the United States Supreme Court, as well as that of his own District Court. Had it not been for the tireless efforts of my attorneys, who fought gallantly, he may well have succeeded. Through their efforts, an emergency panel of the Sixth Circuit Court convened and issued a stay of execution around 6:30 p.m.

Not to be outdone, Ohio Governor George Voinovich personally contacted his friend Ohio Attorney General Lee Fisher to form a pact and went to the United States Supreme Court, asking them to dissolve the stay of execution and order my murder to occur as scheduled. This move was purely political, both of them having had political aspirations with elections coming up, knowing how profitable it would be jumping on the "Kill us quick" bandwagon.

After the U.S. Supreme Court in its entirety had been convened, they declined to lift the stay of execution at approximately 11:30 p.m. Everyone breathed a great sigh of relief, including, I might add, the correctional officers that had been present during the whole ordeal. Around 12:20 a.m. Tuesday morning, I was again escorted, however this time back to Death Row. Again the corridors were filled with loud cheers and good wishes, but it was when I arrived back on the "Row" where I received the most thunderous ovation. Everyone had been following the events closely as they unfolded over the TV and radio, and were all aware that I was coming back.

In the aftermath of Judge Carl Rubin's machinations with my case, he was removed from further involvement. This indicates and validates my previously held suspicions that he was overtly prejudicial towards me and my case, and to all Death Row prisoners, and was losing his judicial temperament. To him, the bench from which he's supposed to make decisions based upon law had instead become a soapbox, upon which he had climbed to orate his personal convictions! For those who are chomping at the bit for my death, complaining about the length of time my appeal was taking, it doesn't matter whether I'm innocent or not—all they want is to have their bloodlust sated. Nothing else matters, damn justice, "Give us the body" they cry.

Many people have written and asked what it's like being on Death Row, being sent to the Death House, and coming within 30 minutes of being murdered by the state. Why I refused to eat my "last meal," and why I chose the electric chair instead of lethal injection. I will try to answer these questions based on my experience, as I'm sure it differs from some others who have been as fortunate as myself. To walk into the very Jaws of the Beast, and walk out again. Sadly this has not been the case for many throughout this country that are similarly situated.

Being on Death Row, in and of itself, is a form of death. The environment sucks the life from you, and the passing of a single day at times can be but the blink of an eye, or as long as a heartbreaking life. Then there's the drudgery, the soul-wrenching monotony of staring at the same steel and concrete, the same people, ad nauseam. Being taken to the Death House is, in a way, a relief. Finally one is afforded the opportunity to confront one's killers, who cowardly hide behind the mask of shamelessness. To look into their eyes, smell their raw fear, and feel one's own strength being pitted against the ultimate sanction—Death.

As for the so-called last meal and my refusal to eat it and other meals, as I said earlier, years of conditioned paranoia, coupled with the exigencies of events going on around me, made eating the furthest thing from my mind.

I chose the electric chair because I refuse to give any credence to the state's attempt to contrive a rationale for its murders, by offering a lethal injection as a "more humane" form of murder. If they were going to kill me, I was intent upon making it as ghastly as possible for all that bore witness to it.

What went through my mind during those 36 hours were thoughts of my woman, people that I care about and love, and what my death would do to them. I was hoping for the best, and expecting the worst. Those 36 hours were devoted to the ones that I care about and love. I had to keep my wits about myself, because as I saw it, it was on me to give the ones I love and care about strength. I had to maintain courage in the face of adversity, so that the ones I care about and love would not have a burden that was over-bearing. Their love and support had sustained me all this time, and it was my turn to show them and give them strength.

There is a plague in this country that is being controlled and manipulated by politicians, judges, prosecutors, police, professional victims and victims' rights groups. Until society faces what's really going on in this country and starts wanting real answers for what's really going on in our streets, a number of innocent people are going to be put to death, or imprisoned for the rest of their lives.

This attitude of Lock Them Up and Kill Them is not the answer. Who do you think are going to be the ones filling our Death Rows, prisons and jails? Open your eyes before it's too late. The future of this society is at stake until *you* the *people* take off your blindfolds and look at the real problems, dealing with them rather than sweeping them under the rug with a quick fix that has never worked. Crime is nothing new, the way it is dealt with is a reflection of the society we live in. The reflection I see is a holocaust against the poor and less fortunate.

To all the brother and sisters, mothers and fathers who are on Death Row, or in jails and prisons throughout this country, or struggling to get through the day to put food on the table: Stay strong and don't give up. Stop turning on each other and stand united against the oppressors and raise your voices in unity!

Columbus Free Press
January 1995

Execution Only Creates More Victims

By Kim Hamer

Nineteen years ago my big brother awoke to a horrible nightmare. At a young stage of his life, when others his age dreamed of their futures, he was burdened with the weight of the world. Johnny became a socially accepted sacrifice—an expendable pawn in the furtherance of self-serving political and financial aspirations.

If Johnny's attorneys were given more time they would have exposed the improprieties and the crimes committed by the Hamilton County Prosecutor's Office in order to obtain a conviction and sentence him to death. I realize it is often heard from others in his situation that they are all innocent. These claims are often taken with a grain of salt. This can no longer be an acceptable practice. Too much evidence has shown that men and women have been wrongfully convicted and executed or imprisoned by the state.

But, when this happens, no one is accountable for knowingly permitting it. This tragic miscarriage of justice burdens every citizen of the United States and does not exclude the state of Ohio from becoming the death machine. But a federal judge of the Sixth Circuit Court, along with many others who have studied this case, conclude that there has been a major breakdown in the judicial system.

Today I ask God, for whom all things are possible, to help turn negatives into positives and anger into self-energy. Johnny's right to be courageous and turn hatred into love would be denied.

May we take this time out to remember that Johnny was an example of a negative to positive transformation during his premature, extinguished life. The transformation which Johnny experienced was what we call God's miracle and blessing.

I have come to the conclusion that my big brother, and everyone's brothers and sisters that have been put to death within our "self-serving laws," and the people of Ohio have made a severe mistake. This would never happen if the people who elected these officials to office would take the time to examine the political and financial aspirations of elected officials. However people do not, thinking that our justice system is sincere and making the choice of leaving the door wide open for the corruption inherent in our criminal justice system. Johnny died for political and financial gains. But, John William Byrd Jr. did not die in vain. You as the public could be walking in my shoes. I wish this on no one. It is time for the public to wake up and stand tall. Scream to abolish the death penalty.

When I was 15 years old my brother Johnny was put on Death Row for something he did not do. He was 19 years old at the time. Johnny, my family and I have had to live through Death Row for 19 years and then they executed him. Murdered him. We were allowed to have a half-hour

contact visit with Johnny the day before execution and that
was very hard, especially seeing what it was doing to our
mother and family.

On the morning of the execution, around 6:30 a.m., we
were allowed a half hour to see Johnny behind bars. What
could I say to my brother at a time like this, not knowing
if I would ever see him alive again? At around 8:30 a.m. we
were no longer allowed to visit with him. My mother,
myself and four other family members had to sit and wait
to see if he would get a stay of execution. When Johnny's
attorney walked into the very small room with my family
it was around 9:55 a.m. They said he was denied; there was
nothing else they could do. There are no words possible to
explain what our family and Johnny had to endure from
that moment on.

Then, while I was trying to comfort our mother, the
warden came back into that very small room to say Johnny
was pronounced dead at 10:09 a.m. From that moment on,
our lives have changed forever. Our mother would not
leave the prison until Johnny's body was taken out of the
prison.

The very next morning I had to go view and claim my
brother's body. That few days in my life will be with me
forever. Everyday I see how our mother hurts, and that is
what pains me even more. But I catch myself thinking of
all the talks I had with Johnny over the phone. "Be the best
that you can be and always stay strong," was always what
my big brother advised me. The death penalty only creates
other victims.

My brother chose electrocution as his manner of death.
I asked him, "Why?" His exact words were, "Sis, if they are
going to murder me, let us show them for what it really is."

And he meant how cruel the death penalty is. So, Governor Taft banned the electric chair. But still I see the eyes of people who believe in the death penalty and think lethal injection is OK. Murder is murder no matter how you look at it. The death penalty is murder. No matter how someone is executed, it is still murder.

I have vowed my life to never give up. No family should have to suffer the way my family has and other families that have someone on Death Row or has lost a loved one due to the death penalty. How do we explain to our children that killing is wrong when our own state murders people guilty or innocent?

About 20 minutes after Johnny's execution I was interviewed in the Lucasville prison only so many feet away from Johnny's limp, dead body. And I told the media that killing my brother has not silenced him, it has only made his voice louder and stronger through me. That is why I say in a few months in Hamilton County the shit is about to hit the fan.

Like Johnny said, it is time to show the death penalty for what it really is. No one is God and should make the decision to kill in the name of justice. It is time to abolish the death penalty. Do not kill in my name.

Speech given at International Human Rights Day rally
in front of the FBI Building, Columbus, Ohio
December 10, 2002

Clemency Could Correct Courts' Errors

BY BIANCA JAGGER

February 12, 2002

Governor Bob Taft
Office of the Governor
30th Floor
77 South High Street
Columbus, OH 43215

Dear Governor Taft,

John Byrd was convicted and sentenced to death for the murder of convenience store clerk Monte Tewksbury. As noted by Sixth Circuit Judge Nathanial R. Jones, John Byrd's conviction was derived from "unpardonable constitutional improprieties." He added that the court's validation of these improprieties was "an intolerable abandonment of substantive and procedural principles deeply rooted in Anglo-Saxon and American constitutional jurisprudence."

On April 17, 1983, Monte Tewksbury, 40, was wounded during a robbery of the convenience store where he worked. He was stabbed once, lived long enough to describe the robbers as two masked men, and died two hours later. At about that time, police stopped a van with John Byrd, John Brewer and William Woodall inside. All three were charged with murder, with Byrd charged as the actual killer, making him alone liable for the death penalty. Since his arrest, John Byrd has maintained his innocence. The others were tried separately and received prison terms. John Byrd received the death penalty

For 16 years, John Brewer has confessed in sworn affidavits that *he committed the murder that John Byrd is condemned to die for.* There is no physical or scientific evidence that places John Byrd at the crime scene: no fingerprints, shoe prints, or hair. Furthermore, the shoeprint found on the counter at the site of the stabbing was John Brewer's. This supports his confession that he murdered Monte Tewksbury.

Furthermore, the state's key witness, Ronald Armstead, a jailhouse snitch, perjured himself when he testified against Byrd. Without this testimony, detailing a purported confession by John Byrd, the State could not have convicted him of capital murder since the state had no other evidence, physical or otherwise, linking John Byrd to the murder.

Sixth Circuit Judge Nathanial R. Jones noted that "the prosecution did not disclose star witness Ronald Armstead's parole records and pending charges. This evidence would have revealed that, at the time of Byrd's trial, Armstead had a pending parole violation hearing where he faced the possibility of three to 15 years of imprisonment."

The questions raised in John Byrd's case are identical to many of those cases in Illinois which resulted in the release of 13 innocent men from Death Row before Governor

Ryan called for a moratorium on all executions to prevent a wrongful execution.

We also stress the fact that, at the time of this writing, 99 wrongfully convicted men throughout the United States have been released from Death Row. Some were exonerated on appeal, some were granted clemency by the governor, and some were released through the work of persons outside of the justice system.

Many of those innocent were initially convicted and sentenced to death through the use of jailhouse snitches. Ronald Armstead is such a snitch, who was released shortly after trial and has not been heard from since.

Although the legal system has upheld John Byrd's death sentence, there is certainly not clear and convincing evidence of his guilt. Clemency is a constitutional power granted to correct grave errors in the courts. The execution of John Byrd will be a tragic miscarriage of justice.

We hope that you reconsider your prior decision and grant clemency to John Byrd.

Respectfully,
Bianca Jagger
Member, Executive Director's Leadership Council
Amnesty International USA

Affidavit

By Bob Fitrakis

1. My name is Robert J. Fitrakis and I reside at 1240 Bryden Rd., Columbus, Ohio. I give this affidavit based upon my personal knowledge.

2. I hold a Ph.D. in political science.

3. I am employed at the Columbus State Community College as a Professor of Political Science.

4. I am a professional journalist with a regular column in *Columbus Alive*.

5. I am currently registered and in attendance at the Ohio State University in its school of law working toward a Juris Doctor degree.

6. I have authored publications and received awards, fellowships and grants as set forth in the attached page 4 of my curriculum vitae.

7. I have reviewed trial transcripts, news reports and other extensive materials related to the criminal prosecution and underlying criminal incident for which John Byrd is currently scheduled to be executed. I have also spoken with John Byrd and other witnesses.

8. I have published extensively alone and in collaboration with Martin Yant in regard to the facts and circumstances of the John Byrd criminal matter. In the course of

doing so I have been in a regular dialogue with other journalists and writers interested in this subject as well as with members of the public at large, including but not limited to members of the religious community in Columbus and throughout the state of Ohio.

9. Based upon my review of the Byrd matter in my capacity as an investigative reporter, political scientist and law student, I have formed opinions to a reasonable degree of certainly within each of the fields in which I have expertise.

10. In my opinion John Byrd is innocent of the capital murder charge pursuant to which his execution is currently scheduled.

11. In my opinion if John Byrd were to be retried upon the same charge of capital murder today, based upon the evidence now available, he could not be convicted beyond a reasonable doubt by a jury of his peers.

12. In my opinion, a reasonable and objective prosecutor would not proceed with a new prosecution of John Byrd on the capital murder charge for which he is now scheduled to be executed.

13. On the current state of the evidence there is, in my opinion, an absence of probable cause to believe that John Byrd is guilty of the capital murder for which he is scheduled to be executed.

Further affiant sayeth naught.
Robert J. Fitrakis

*Sworn and subscribed before a Notary Public
this 15th day of February 2002.*

About The Author

Bob Fitrakis is a political science professor at Columbus State Community College, where he won the Distinguished Teaching Award in 1991, and a frequent speaker on political, labor and social policy issues at national academic and political conferences. He earned his Ph.D. in Political Science from Wayne State University and his J.D. from the Ohio State University Law School.

As a columnist and investigative reporter for the weekly alternative newspaper *Columbus Alive* from 1996 to 2002, Fitrakis won 10 editorial awards from local, state and national journalism associations. In 2002, Fitrakis, Jamie Pietras and Martin Yant won the first-place award for Best Criminal Justice Reporting from the Ohio Society of Professional Journalists for their dogged investigation into the John Byrd death penalty case.

Fitrakis is the executive director of the Columbus Institute for Contemporary Journalism and has published the *Columbus Free Press* since 1992 and acted as the journal's editor since 1993. Fitrakis has co-hosted a news/public affairs program on public access television, and he hosts a weekly call-in talk radio program on WVKO-AM.

Fitrakis is the author of *The Idea of Democratic Socialism in America and the Decline of the Socialist Party* (Garland

Publishers, 1993). His previous volume in this series, *The Fitrakis Files: Spooks, Nukes & Nazis* (Columbus Alive/CICJ), was published in 2003.

He has won various community awards for his journalism and activism, among them the 1998 award for Outstanding Community Journalism from the Police Officers for Equal Rights, the 2001 Golden Ruler Award—the highest honor the Columbus Board of Education bestows—"in acknowledgement of his efforts as a strong advocate for minority and disadvantaged students, a voice for adequate public funding, and a champion of ethical school governance," and the 2003 Selma Walker Award for Lifetime Achievement in Human Rights Activism presented by the Native American Indian Center of Central Ohio.

Fitrakis was a candidate for U.S. Congress in 1992, for the Columbus School Board in 1995, and for Columbus City Council in 2003. He was a ward representative on the Franklin County Democratic Party Central Committee from 1996 to 2000. He served on the Africentric School Advisory Board for the Columbus Public Schools and worked with the West High School College Preparation Program. He currently serves on the city of Columbus' Near East Area Commission.

Printed in the United States
70996LV00001B/154-159